Math Mammoth Grade 2 Skills Review Workbook

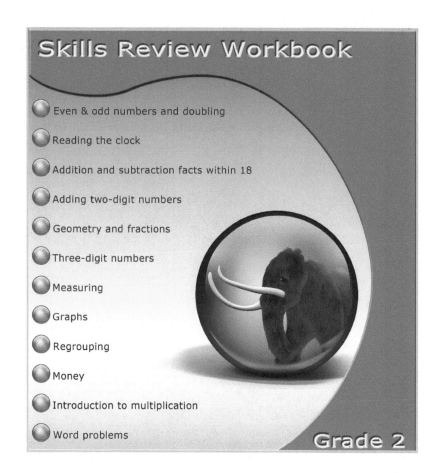

Skills Review Workbook

- Even & odd numbers and doubling
- Reading the clock
- Addition and subtraction facts within 18
- Adding two-digit numbers
- Geometry and fractions
- Three-digit numbers
- Measuring
- Graphs
- Regrouping
- Money
- Introduction to multiplication
- Word problems

Grade 2

By Maria Miller

Contents

Chapter 4: Regrouping in Addition

Chapter 5: Geometry and Fractions

Chapter 6: Three-Digit Numbers

Foreword

Math Mammoth Grade 2 Skills Review Workbook has been created to complement the lessons in *Math Mammoth Grade 2* complete curriculum. It gives the students practice in reviewing what they have already studied, so the concepts and skills will become more established in their memory.

These review worksheets are designed to provide a spiral review of the concepts in the curriculum. This means that after a concept or skill has been studied in the main curriculum, it is then reviewed repeatedly over time in several different worksheets of this book.

This book is divided into chapters, according to the corresponding chapters in the *Math Mammoth Grade 2* curriculum. You can choose exactly when to use the worksheets within the chapter, and how many of them to use. Not all students need all of these worksheets to help them keep their math skills fresh, so please vary the amount of worksheets you assign your student(s) according to their needs.

Each worksheet is designed to be one page, and includes a variety of exercises in a fun way without becoming too long and tedious. We have created a spreadsheet document that lists the lessons spiraled in each worksheet. This document is included with the digital (download) version. You can also download it at the following link:

https://www.mathmammoth.com/skills_review_workbooks/guides/Skills_Review_Grade2_Spiraling_Guide.xls

The printed answer key can be purchased separately or in the digital download version it is included in the zip file.

I wish you success in teaching math!

Maria Miller, the author

Skills Review 1

1. Color the flower petals using the color guide. Then color the rest of the picture.

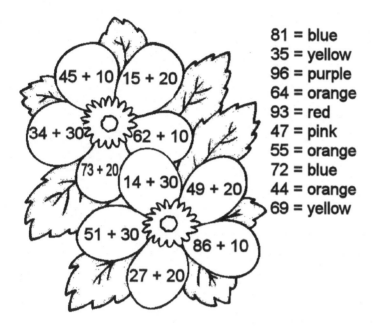

81 = blue
35 = yellow
96 = purple
64 = orange
93 = red
47 = pink
55 = orange
72 = blue
44 = orange
69 = yellow

2. Add. In some of these problems you need to <u>make a new ten</u> with some of the little dots.

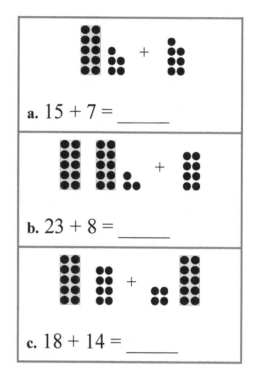

a. $15 + 7 =$ _____

b. $23 + 8 =$ _____

c. $18 + 14 =$ _____

3. Sarah had 33 stickers. Then Kim and Becky each gave her more stickers, so now she has 40.

   a. Kim gave Sarah 4 stickers. How many did Becky give her?

   b. Sarah used 20 of her stickers to decorate a birthday card. How many stickers does she have left?

4. Subtract.

a.	7	6	**b.**	5	8	**c.**	9	9	**d.**	6	5
−	3	1	−	4	5	−	7	4	−	2	2

Skills Review 2

1. Skip-count backwards.

a. 86, 84, 82, _____, _____, 76, _____, _____, _____, _____

b. _____, _____, _____, _____, 65, 55, 45, _____, 25, _____

2. Solve.

a. $\boxed{} - 6 = 2$	b. $\boxed{} - 5 = 5$	c. $12 - \boxed{} = 1$

3. Mark and Brendan were collecting pine cones. Brendan found seventeen pine cones and Mark found twelve.

a. How many fewer pine cones did Mark find than Brendan?

b. How many pine cones did the two boys find, in total?

4. Add or subtract.

a.	b.	c.	d.
$9 - 9 = $ _____	$30 + 5 + 3 = $ _____	$50 - 1 = $ _____	$20 + $ _____ $= 35$

5. Circle three numbers that form a fact family. Write the problems on the lines below.

a. 9 6 5 7 3	b. 50 70 90 30 80
____ + ____ = ____	____ + ____ = ____
____ + ____ = ____	____ + ____ = ____
____ − ____ = ____	____ − ____ = ____
____ − ____ = ____	____ − ____ = ____

Skills Review 3

1. Complete the number puzzle.

13	+		=	43
+				
20	+	56	=	
=		−		−
				40
		=		=
	+	26	=	

2. Add or subtract.

a.
```
  7 9
- 4 5
─────
```

b.
```
  3 4
+ 5 2
─────
```

c.
```
  6 8
+ 3 0
─────
```

d.
```
  8 8
- 6 7
─────
```

3. Draw lines to match the problems that are from the same fact family.

$7 + 3 = 10$ $4 + 5 = 9$ $10 - 2 = 8$

$6 - 4 = 2$ $10 - 8 = 2$ $5 + 4 = 9$

$9 - 5 = 4$ $2 + 4 = 6$ $10 - 7 = 3$

$8 + 2 = 10$ $3 + 7 = 10$ $6 - 2 = 4$

4. Solve the word problems.

a. Bill, Matt, and Eric were picking oranges in an orchard.
Matt picked 30 oranges, Eric picked 20, and Bill picked 25.
How many oranges did they pick in total?

b. Marsha needs to make 48 cupcakes for a school picnic. So far, she has
made 30 cupcakes. How many more would she still need to make?

Surprise! Marsha's friend Nancy showed up at Marsha's house and gave
her 10 cupcakes. How many more cupcakes does Marsha need to make now?

Skills Review 4

1.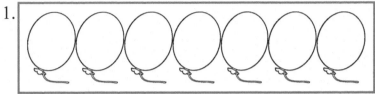

Color...

...the third balloon from the left yellow.

...the seventh balloon from the right purple.

...the first balloon from the right green.

...the fourth balloon from the left red.

...the sixth balloon from the right pink.

...the second balloon from the right orange.

...the fifth balloon from the left brown.

2. Write problems to form a fact family.

T	T	T	T

_____ + _____ = _____

_____ + _____ = _____

_____ − _____ = _____

_____ − _____ = _____

3. Solve the word problems.

a. Vanessa was gathering chicken eggs on her grandpa's farm. She found 20 eggs in the chicken coop, 7 eggs in the barn, and 3 eggs in Grandpa's old hat! How many eggs did she gather, in total?

b. Luke had $78. Then, he bought a puzzle for $12 and a flashlight for $15. How much money does he have left?

Luke wants to buy a camera that costs $54. Does he have enough money left to buy it?

If yes, how much money does he have left?

If no, how much more money does he need?

4. Skip-count.

a. 42, 44, _____, _____, _____, 52, _____, _____, _____

b. 105, 100, _____, _____, 85, _____, _____, _____, _____

Skills Review 5

1. Can two people share these things evenly? If yes, circle EVEN. If not, circle ODD.

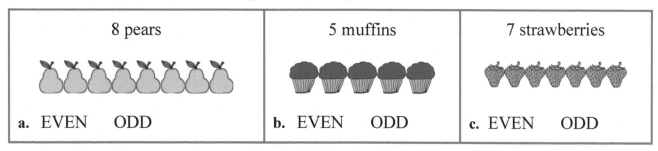

8 pears	5 muffins	7 strawberries
a. EVEN ODD	b. EVEN ODD	c. EVEN ODD

2. Find the number that goes into the shape.

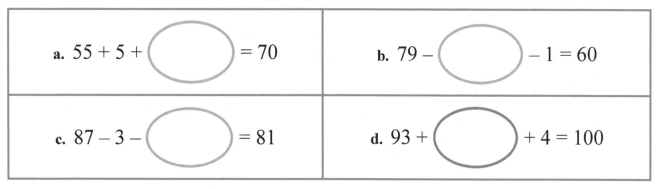

a. $55 + 5 + \bigcirc = 70$

b. $79 - \bigcirc - 1 = 60$

c. $87 - 3 - \bigcirc = 81$

d. $93 + \bigcirc + 4 = 100$

3. Sharon caught 17 fireflies and Kayla caught 12.
   How many more fireflies did Sharon catch than Kayla?

   Brett caught 28 fireflies! Did he catch more fireflies
   than Sharon and Kayla did altogether?

4. Carmen baked 14 muffins and shared them equally
   with her neighbor. How many muffins did each one
   get?

5. Which ball is colored? Write the correct ordinal number on the line.

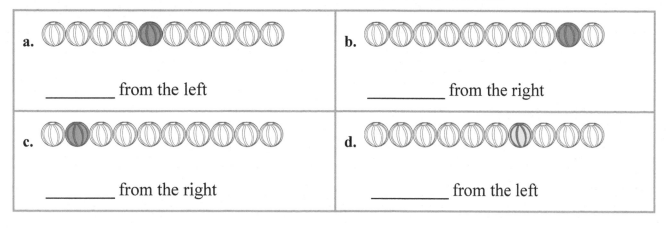

a.	b.
_____ from the left	_____ from the right
c.	d.
_____ from the right	_____ from the left

11

Skills Review 6

1. Add the doubles in the boxes.

    a. Double 12   **b.** 23 + 23   **c.** Double 44   **d.** Double 31

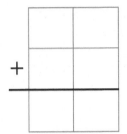 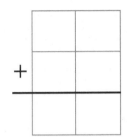 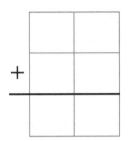

2. Can you share these amounts evenly with a friend? If yes, write "E" or "even" in the last column. If not, write "O" or "odd". You may use rocks, beans, or other small items as a visual aid.

Balloons	Share evenly?	Even or odd?
18		
7		
11		

Balloons	Share evenly?	Even or odd?
5		
12		
14		

3. Leila picked 12 yellow flowers, 10 red flowers, and 8 pink flowers. She shared them equally with her friend Katrina. How many flowers did each girl get?

4. Mom cooked 12 pancakes for her three children. Jim ate 4 pancakes and Sandra ate 3 pancakes, and Adrian ate the rest. How many pancakes did Adrian eat?

5. Add or subtract.

a.	b.	c.	d.
80 − ____ = 75	20 + 5 + 5 = _____	14 + ____ = 20	68 − ____ = 61

1. Use letters from the given word to make a new word.

S K A T E B O A R D

___ ___ ___ ___ ___
6th   8th   2nd   5th   10th

2. Solve the subtractions, and write a matching addition for each.

a. ____ + ____ = ____

   30 − 6 = _____

b. ____ + ____ = ____

   16 − 8 = _____

3. Complete the doubles chart.

9 + 9 = _____

10 + 10 = _____

11 + 11 = _____

12 + 12 = _____

13 + 13 = _____

14 + 14 = _____

15 + 15 = _____

4. Color using the color guide. Then color the rest of the picture.

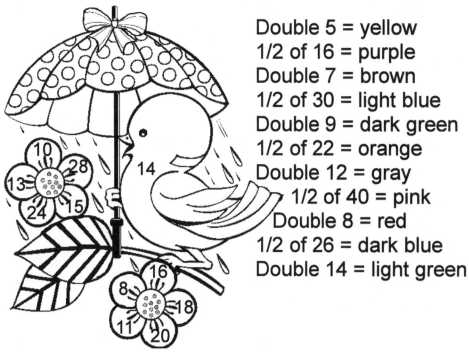

Double 5 = yellow
1/2 of 16 = purple
Double 7 = brown
1/2 of 30 = light blue
Double 9 = dark green
1/2 of 22 = orange
Double 12 = gray
1/2 of 40 = pink
Double 8 = red
1/2 of 26 = dark blue
Double 14 = light green

5. Subtract 3 from each number on the bottom. Notice the pattern!

		7										
6	8	10	12	14	16	18	20	22	24	26	28	30

13

Skills Review 8

1. Find the number that goes into the shape.

a. $60 + 10 + \bigcirc = 100$	**b.** $22 + \bigcirc + 2 = 30$

2. Circle the odd numbers with a blue crayon and the even numbers with a red crayon.

15	11	4	10
2	6	9	12
5	14	1	8
13	7	16	3

3. Write each number as a double of some other number.

a. $20 = \underline{\hspace{2cm}} + \underline{\hspace{2cm}}$

b. $14 = \underline{\hspace{2cm}} + \underline{\hspace{2cm}}$

c. $30 = \underline{\hspace{2cm}} + \underline{\hspace{2cm}}$

d. $12 = \underline{\hspace{2cm}} + \underline{\hspace{2cm}}$

4. Solve the word problems.

a. Mrs. Johnson has 20 girls and 17 boys in her class. How many students does she have in total?

On Friday, 5 of Mrs. Johnson's students were sick and didn't come to school. How many students came to school that day?

b. Peter and Kyle picked 40 strawberries. If they shared them equally, how many would each boy get?

Oh no! Peter's dog, Sparky, found the strawberries and gobbled up 5 of them. How many strawberries are left? Can the boys share them equally?

c. Cheryl has 55 coins in her coin collection, and Karen has 40. How many more coins does Cheryl have than Karen?

Skills Review 9

1. Draw a line through these shapes and divide them into two halves. Color one half.

  a.   **b.**   **c.**   **d.**   **e.**

2. Marissa has 18 colored pencils and her
sister Kayla has 13. How many more
colored pencils does Marissa have than
Kayla?

   Marissa gave Kayla 5 of her colored pencils.
   How many colored pencils does Kayla have
   now?

   Is that an odd number or an even number?

3. Which additions and subtractions equal the number in the middle of the flower?
Color them.

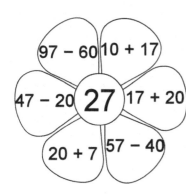 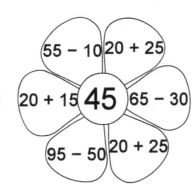 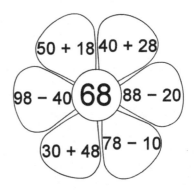

4. Add in the boxes to find the double of these numbers.

    a. $33 + 33$ **b.** Double 12   **c.** $21 + 21$ **d.** Double 44

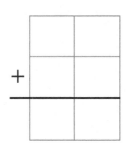 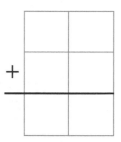

Skills Review 10

1. Write the time in two ways: using the expressions *o'clock* or *half past*, and with numbers.

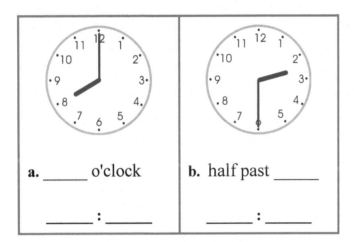

a. _____ o'clock

_____ : _____

b. half past _____

_____ : _____

2. Complete the problems to form a fact family.

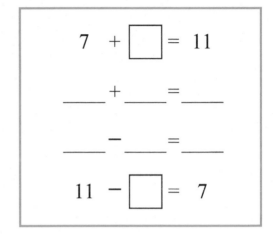

$$7 + \boxed{} = 11$$

$$\underline{} + \underline{} = \underline{}$$

$$\underline{} - \underline{} = \underline{}$$

$$11 - \boxed{} = 7$$

3. Divide the dots into two EQUAL groups. Find half of the total.

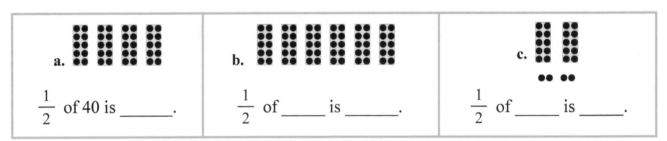

a. $\frac{1}{2}$ of 40 is _____.

b. $\frac{1}{2}$ of _____ is _____.

c. $\frac{1}{2}$ of _____ is _____.

4. Matt had $79. He bought a clock for $30 and a set of drawing pencils for $20.

   a. How much money did he have left?

   b. Matt's grandma gave him $50 for his birthday. How much money does he have now?

5. Subtract 4 from each number on the bottom. Notice the pattern!

11	16	21	26	31	36	41	46	51	56	61	66	71

Skills Review 11

1. Circle.

   a. The fourth fish from the left.

   b. The seventh fish from the right.

   c. The eighth snail from the left.

   d. The fifth snail from the right.

2. Write the time an hour later.

Now it is:	**a.** 8:30	**b.** 2:00
An hour later, it is:		

3. Write the time a half-hour later.

Now it is:	**a.** 12:30	**b.** 9:00
A half-hour later, it is:		

4. Add or subtract.

a.
```
    7  8
 -  4  5
_____
```

b.
```
    3  2
 +  5  5
_____
```

c.
```
    9  6
 -  7  3
_____
```

d.
```
    2  7
 +  6  0
_____
```

Puzzle Corner — How many different solutions can you find for this puzzle? Find at least two. All numbers are whole tens.

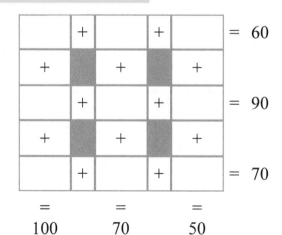

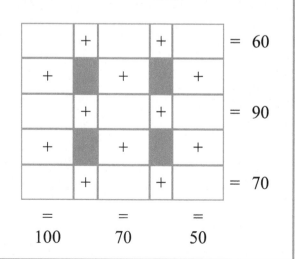

Skills Review 12

1. Find the number that is missing.
   Then write a matching subtraction.

a.   13 + ____ = 19

   _____ – _____ = _____

b. ____ + 82 = 90

   _____ – _____ = _____

2. Write two different missing-number problems using two-digit numbers. Then let your friend solve them.

a.

b.

3. Solve the word problems.

a. Andrew, Susan, and Conrad played tag in the yard for an hour. If they started playing at 5:30, what time did they finish?

   When the children finished their game, Mom told them that supper would be ready in half an hour. What time did they eat supper?

b. Peyton and Alan earned $24 raking leaves. If they share the money equally, how much money will each boy get?

c. Mom is buying notebooks for Rachel and Martina. If each girl needs 7 notebooks, how many notebooks does Mom need to buy?

4. Write the time.

a. _____ : _____   b. _____ : _____   c. _____ : _____   d. _____ : _____

Skills Review 13

1. Find the missing numbers.

a.	$\boxed{} - 8 = 8$
b.	$90 - \boxed{} = 10$
c.	$\boxed{} - 3 = 13$
d.	$70 - \boxed{} = 20$

2. Write the time that the clock shows, and the time 5 minutes later.

	a. 	**b.**
	_____ : _____	_____ : _____
5 min. later →	_____ : _____	_____ : _____

3. Add or subtract.

a.	**b.**	**c.**
$35 + 20 + 5 = \underline{}$	$72 + 4 + 3 = \underline{}$	$86 - 10 - 3 = \underline{}$

4. Megan had 16 crayons. Then, she gave half of her crayons to her little sister. How many crayons does Megan have left?

5. Sebastian found 5 toy cars under his bed, 7 in the basement, and 3 in the doghouse. How many toy cars did Sebastian find?

   Can Sebastian share his toy cars equally with his friend Josh?

6. Color.

a. The fourth frog from the left.   **b.** The second duck from the right.

Skills Review 14

1. Skip-count by threes starting at 3.
   Color these numbers pink.

2. Skip-count by threes starting at 4.
   Color these numbers light blue.

1	2	3	4	5	6	7	8	9	10
11	12	13	14	15	16	17	18	19	20
21	22	23	24	25	26	27	28	29	30
31	32	33	34	35	36	37	38	39	40
41	42	43	44	45	46	47	48	49	50
51	52	53	54	55	56	57	58	59	60
61	62	63	64	65	66	67	68	69	70
71	72	73	74	75	76	77	78	79	80
81	82	83	84	85	86	87	88	89	90
91	92	93	94	95	96	97	98	99	100

3. Allison planted 37 flower seeds, Eric planted 30
   and Vanessa planted 10. How many flower seeds
   did they plant in total?

   Bad dog! Mitzi dug holes ALL OVER in the flower
   garden! After that only 25 seeds sprouted.
   How many seeds didn't sprout?

4. Mom needs to bake the meatloaf for one hour.
   If she puts it in the oven at 4:30, what time
   will it be done?

   Dad didn't get home from work until half an
   hour after the meatloaf was done. What time
   did he get home?

5. How many minutes it is till the next whole hour?

a.

It is _____ minutes

till 3 o'clock.

b.

It is _____ minutes

till _____ o'clock.

c.

It is _____ minutes

till _____ o'clock.

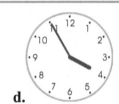

d.

It is _____ minutes

till _____ o'clock.

Skills Review 15

1. Put the letters in order to make a word.
   The first letter of your new word is "S."

E	U	L	R	W	S	O	N	S	F
8th	2nd	5th	9th	7th	1st	6th	3rd	10th	4th

   <u>S</u> ___ ___ ___ ___ ___ ___ ___ ___ ___

2. The Jackson family went on a picnic.
   They arrived at the park at 12:00 and left
   at 5:00. How many hours did they spend
   in the park?

3. Angela and Blake helped their grandma clean
   her house. They started cleaning at 7:00 and
   it took them three hours. What time did they
   finish?

4. Find the missing numbers in the additions and subtractions.

   a.
   ```
        1
   +       3
   ─────────
     2    6
   ```

   b.
   ```
             6
   −    4
   ─────────
     5    2
   ```

   c.
   ```
   +    5    4
   ─────────
     9    7
   ```

   d.
   ```
     8    7
   −
   ─────────
     4    1
   ```

5. Write the time.

a. _____ : _____   b. _____ : _____   c. _____ : _____   d. _____ : _____

Skills Review 16

1. Divide the items into two EQUAL groups. Write an addition. Find half of the total.

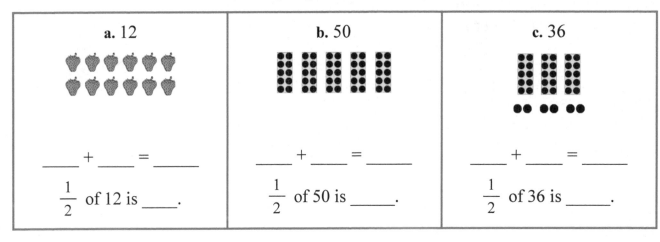

a. 12	b. 50	c. 36
____ + ____ = ____	____ + ____ = ____	____ + ____ = ____
$\frac{1}{2}$ of 12 is ____ .	$\frac{1}{2}$ of 50 is ____ .	$\frac{1}{2}$ of 36 is ____ .

2. Fill in the month before and after the given month.

	June	
	September	

3. Grandpa gave Jesse and Garth a bag of 46
   marbles. If the two boys share the marbles
   equally, how many will each one get?

   A crow stole 8 of the boys' marbles.
   How many marbles do they have left?
   Can they still share the marbles equally?

4. Mrs. Anderson baked 64 chocolate chip cookies
   for a bake sale, but she only sold half of them.
   How many cookies did she have left?

5. How many hours is it?

from	8 AM	6 AM	9 AM	12 AM	3 AM
to	2 PM	5 PM	3 PM	9 PM	7 PM
hours					

Skills Review 17

1. Imagine that today's date is August 12th.

   a. What was the date one week ago?

   _____

   b. What is the date two weeks later than August 12th?

   _____

August						
Su	Mo	Tu	We	Th	Fr	Sa
	1	2	3	4	5	6
7	8	9	10	11	12	13
14	15	16	17	18	19	20
21	22	23	24	25	26	27
28	29	30	31			

2. Add or subtract the same number each time.

   a. $+ 20$

77	_____
19	_____
20	_____
43	_____

   b. $- 10$

90	_____
32	_____
69	_____
56	_____

   c. $+ 5$

72	_____
83	_____
45	_____
14	_____

3. Mary has 15 feathers, 15 pretty rocks, and 10 pine cones in her treasure collection. How many items does she have in total?

   Mary's mom gave her 20 seashells. How many items does she have in her treasure collection now?

4. Look at the calendar at the top of this page. What day of the week is...

   ...August 10th? _____ ...August 27th? _____

5. Write the time using the **hours : minutes** way. Use your practice clock to help.

a. 5 past 12	**b.** 20 till 9	**c.** 10 past 6	**d.** half-past 2
_____ : _____	_____ : _____	_____ : _____	_____ : _____

23

Skills Review 18

1. Add the given number (10, 20, 30, or 40). In the box below the number, write "E" if the number is even, and "O", if the number is odd.

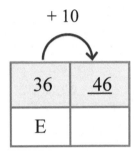
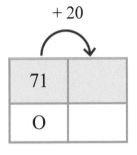
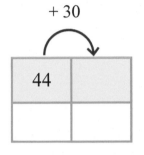
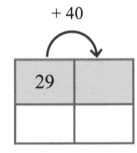

+ 10		+ 20		+ 30		+ 40	
36	46	71		44		29	
E		O					

2. Write the later time.

Time now	7:25	11:55
5 min. later	___ : ___	___ : ___

Time now	1:05	9:50
10 min. later	___ : ___	___ : ___

3. Find the missing numbers in the additions and subtractions.

a.			b.			c.			d.		
				7				6		7	5
+	4	7	−		3	+	4		−		
	8	9		2	6		7	8		3	2

4. Kevin arrived at the zoo at 9:00 and left at 1:00.
   How many hours did he stay at the zoo?

5. Annie invited eighteen children to her birthday
   party. Eleven of the children were girls.
   How many were boys?

6. Subtract.

a.	b.	c.
79 − 10 = _____	32 − 20 = _____	65 − 10 = _____
79 − 20 = _____	32 − 30 = _____	65 − 30 = _____

Skills Review 19

1. Add 4 to each number on the bottom. Notice the pattern!

26	29	32	35	38	41	44	47	50	53

2. Oops! Sophia tried to help Mom put away the dishes and got
   all confused! Mom found 10 bowls in the closet, 8 plates
   in the living room, and 30 spoons in the bathtub! How many
   things did Sophia put away in the wrong place?

3. It is March 21st and Megan is excited because her grandma
   is coming to visit in a week! What is the date that Megan's
   grandma is coming to visit?

   Megan's grandma got sick and didn't come until one week
   later than she had planned. What date did Megan's grandma
   come?

4. Complete the next ten.

a. 96 + _____ = 100	**b.** 42 + _____ = _____	**c.** 74 + _____ = _____

5. Write the time in two ways: using the expressions *o'clock* or *half past*, and with
   numbers.

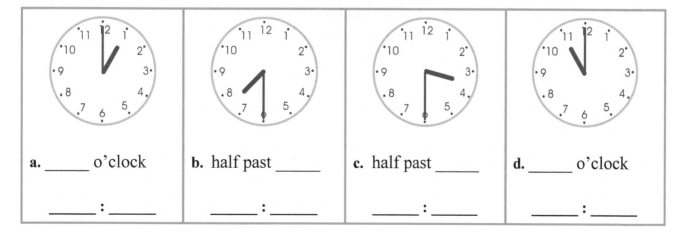

a. _____ o'clock

_____ : _____

b. half past _____

_____ : _____

c. half past _____

_____ : _____

d. _____ o'clock

_____ : _____

Skills Review 20

1. Let's say it is Wednesday. What day of the week will it be...

   a. in 2 days? _____ **b.** in 7 days? _____

   c. in 6 days? _____ **d.** in 4 days? _____

2. Fill in. Imagine that the first number wants to become a ten.

a. $8 + 5 = $ ____	**b.** $9 + 7 = $ ____	**c.** $8 + 6 = $ ____

3. Complete the next whole ten.

a. $22 + $ ____ $+ 3 = 30$	**b.** $74 + $ ____ $+ 2 = 80$	**c.** $91 + $ ____ $+ 6 = 100$

4. Solve the word problems.

   a. Farmer Brown harvested 24 watermelons and shared them equally with his neighbor, Mr. Jefferson. How many watermelons did each one get?

   b. Karen has $15 and her friend Amy has double that amount. How much money do they have together?

   c. Tim was carrying 56 cherries in a basket. Some birds stole 12 of the cherries. Then, Tim dropped the basket and 20 cherries fell out. How many cherries were left in the basket?

5. What is missing?

a. $9 + $ ☐ $= 15$	**b.** $9 + $ ☐ $= 18$	**c.** ☐ $+ 9 = 12$

Skills Review 21

1. Read the clues below and then write each man's name (or initial) below his picture:

_____ _____ _____ _____ _____ _____ _____ _____

The third man from the right is Bob.

The fifth man from the left is Ray.

The second man from the right is Jim.

The fourth man from the left is Sid.

The first man from the right is Max.

The second man from the left is Tom.

The eighth man from the right is Art.

The third man from the left is Don.

2. Complete the puzzle.

	+	5	=	
+				
8	+		=	11
=		+		+
17				
		=		=
	+	12	=	20

3. Mom needs 30 apples to make pies, but she only has 23. How many more apples does she need?

Dad came home from the store with 15 more apples. Mom made the pies. How many apples did Mom have left over?

4. Mike washed the car. He started at 3:30 and finished 1 1/2 hours later. What time did he finish?

5. Write the time using the expressions "past," "till," or "half past."

a. 1:30 _____

b. 7:50 _____

c. 11:25 _____

Skills Review 22

1. Match.

2. Add so that you get 10, 11, and 12.

a.
$8 + \underline{\hspace{2cm}} = 10$
$8 + \underline{\hspace{2cm}} = 11$
$8 + \underline{\hspace{2cm}} = 12$
b.
$6 + \underline{\hspace{2cm}} = 10$
$6 + \underline{\hspace{2cm}} = 11$
$6 + \underline{\hspace{2cm}} = 12$

3. It is June and Zachary is going to visit his Aunt Mary.
   The last time he visited her was 5 months ago.
   During what month did he visit her last?

4. Mom went shopping at the grocery store on September 7th.
   Five days later, she went shopping again. On what date did
   she go shopping?

5. Add 9 to each number on the bottom. Then color the boxes with even numbers green
   and the boxes with odd numbers yellow.

3	10	17	24	31	38	45	52	59	66	73	80	87

Skills Review 23

1. Add or subtract.

a.	b.	c.	d.
48 − ___ = 18	50 + ___ = 75	___ + 37 = 97	87 − 40 = ___

2. On Thursday, Jerry lost his homework and couldn't find it anywhere. Four days later, he finally found it in the refrigerator! On what day of the week did Jerry find his homework?

3. It is December, and Jakob's mom just told him that they are going to visit Hawaii in seven months. In what month are they going to visit Hawaii?

4. Color.

11 = brown
12 = gray
13 = pink
14 = red
15 = yellow
16 = blue
17 = green
18 = orange
19 = purple

5. How many hours is it?

from	5 AM	8 AM	11 AM	2 AM	6 AM
to	7 PM	2 PM	11 PM	12 noon	7 PM
hours					

Skills Review 24

1. Don't write the answers; just practice adding in your head.

$8 + 0 = \square$	$8 + 5 = \square$	$8 + 8 = \square$	$8 + 9 = \square$
$8 + 3 = \square$	$8 + 7 = \square$	$8 + 1 = \square$	$8 + 4 = \square$
$8 + 10 = \square$	$8 + 1 = \square$	$8 + 6 = \square$	$8 + 2 = \square$

2. Andrea picked 8 red roses, 4 yellow roses, and 6 white roses, and shared them equally with her sister. How many roses did each one get?

3. Complete the next whole ten.

a. $22 + \underline{\hspace{1cm}} + 4 = 30$	b. $55 + \underline{\hspace{1cm}} + 2 = 60$	c. $71 + \underline{\hspace{1cm}} + 6 = 80$

4. Subtract.

a.
7	8
− 4	5

b.
9	6
− 5	5

c.
6	5
− 3	2

d.
8	7
− 7	3

5. Write the time that the clock shows, and the time 5 minutes later.

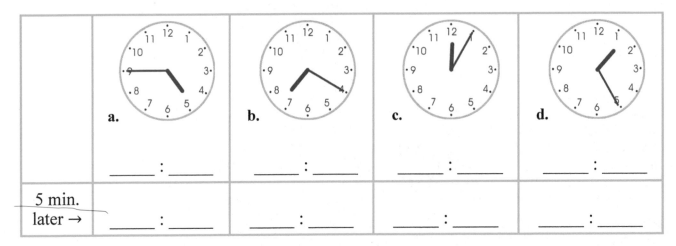

	a. ____ : ____	b. ____ : ____	c. ____ : ____	d. ____ : ____
5 min. later →	____ : ____	____ : ____	____ : ____	____ : ____

1. Mom bakes bread every Friday. What dates will she bake bread during the month of March?

March _____   March _____

March _____   March _____

March
Su Mo Tu We Th Fr Sa
1 2 3 4 5
6 7 8 9 10 11 12
13 14 15 16 17 18 19
20 21 22 23 24 25 26
27 28 29 30 31

2. Starting at the top, count by nines and color a path through the maze!

7	12	9	5	4
11	18	10	14	6
27	15	11	19	16
22	36	20	18	21
23	26	45	27	24
29	31	54	63	32
36	23	39	37	72
42	49	43	81	46
49	41	90	48	42
53	99	47	56	51

3. Fill in the missing numbers.

a.

$8 + \underline{\hphantom{XXX}} = 19$

$6 + \underline{\hphantom{XXX}} = 14$

$7 + \underline{\hphantom{XXX}} = 16$

b.

$\underline{\hphantom{XXX}} + 9 = 15$

$\underline{\hphantom{XXX}} + 6 = 13$

$\underline{\hphantom{XXX}} + 8 = 17$

4. Solve the problems.

a. Rachel's three dogs all had puppies! Cinnamon had eight puppies, Nutmeg had six, and Ginger had two. Rachel sold half of the puppies. How many puppies are left?

b. It is 2:00 and Damian will leave in five hours to go to work. What time will Damian leave?

Skills Review 26

1. Don't write the answers; just practice the sums in your head.

9 + 0 = ☐	9 + 5 = ☐	9 + 9 = ☐	9 + 4 = ☐
9 + 3 = ☐	9 + 6 = ☐	9 + 1 = ☐	9 + 10 = ☐
9 + 7 = ☐	9 + 8 = ☐	9 + 2 = ☐	

2. Write above each shaded number what number it is double of.

6	8	10	12	14	16	18	20	22	24	26	28	30

3. Write the time using the wordings "past" or "till", and using numbers.

a. _____ _____ : _____

b. _____ _____ : _____

c. _____ _____ : _____

Puzzle Corner

Find numbers for the puzzles.

	+		= 80
−	▓	−	
	+		= 30

= 30   = 20

	−		= 50
+	▓	+	
	−		= 20

= 100   = 30

32

1. First subtract enough that you have only 10 left. Then subtract the rest.

a. $14 - 8$	b. $13 - 6$	c. $17 - 9$
/ \	/ \	/ \
$14 - \underline{\quad} - \underline{\quad}$	$13 - \underline{\quad} - \underline{\quad}$	$17 - \underline{\quad} - \underline{\quad}$
$= \underline{\quad}$	$= \underline{\quad}$	$= \underline{\quad}$

2. Bethany needs 40 popsicle sticks for a craft project but she only has 33. How many more popsicle sticks does she need?

  Bethany's mom gave her 24 popsicle sticks. How many popsicle sticks does she have now?

3. Greg has 8 goldfish in one tank and 9 goldfish in another tank. He would like to have 20 in total. How many more goldfish does he need?

4. Let's practice doubles—and doubles plus **one more**!

a. $7 + 7 = \underline{\quad}$	b. $6 + 6 = \underline{\quad}$	c. $9 + 9 = \underline{\quad}$
$7 + 8 = \underline{\quad}$	$6 + 7 = \underline{\quad}$	$9 + 10 = \underline{\quad}$

5. Write the previous and next **whole ten**. Then, circle the ten that is nearer the given number.

a. $\underline{\quad}$, 88, $\underline{\quad}$	b. $\underline{\quad}$, 34, $\underline{\quad}$	c. $\underline{\quad}$, 21, $\underline{\quad}$

6. How many hours is it till midnight?

from	3 PM	8 PM	12 noon	6 AM	2 AM
to	12 midnight	12 midnight	12 midnight	12 midnight	12 midnight
hours					

Skills Review 28

1. Don't write the answers; just practice the sums in your head.

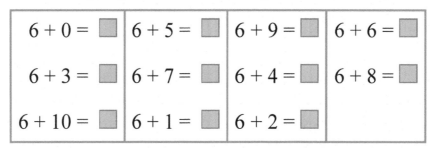

6 + 0 = ☐	6 + 5 = ☐	6 + 9 = ☐	6 + 6 = ☐
6 + 3 = ☐	6 + 7 = ☐	6 + 4 = ☐	6 + 8 = ☐
6 + 10 = ☐	6 + 1 = ☐	6 + 2 = ☐	

2. Write a "*how many more*" addition to find the difference between the numbers.

a. The difference between 15 and 6	**b.** The difference between 8 and 16
6 + _____ = 15	_____ + _____ = 16

3. Find the difference between the numbers.

a. The difference between 12 and 7	**b.** The difference between 50 and 90	**c.** The difference between 19 and 14

4. Carl picked 57 blackberries and put them in his old hat, because he didn't have a bag. But his hat had a hole in it and 20 blackberries fell out. How many blackberries are left in his hat?

   Carl fixed the hole in his hat, and he put the 20 blackberries back in, plus 30 more! How many blackberries does Carl have in his hat now?

5. Circle the clock that shows the time 5 minutes **earlier** than the given time.

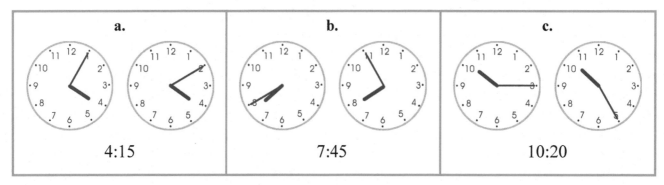

a.	**b.**	**c.**
4:15	7:45	10:20

Skills Review 29

Skills Review 29

1. Fill and color the number rainbow. Then practice the subtraction problems.

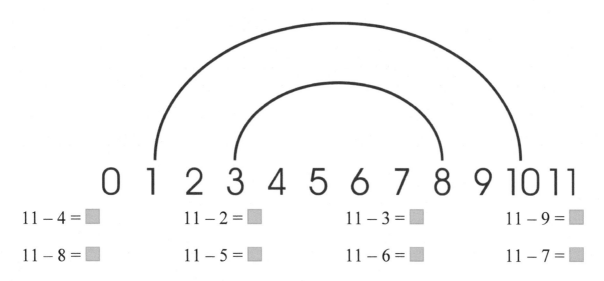

11 − 4 = ▢   11 − 2 = ▢   11 − 3 = ▢   11 − 9 = ▢

11 − 8 = ▢   11 − 5 = ▢   11 − 6 = ▢   11 − 7 = ▢

2. Each flower contains the numbers for *two* sums (such as 8 + 3 = 11 and 6 + 6 = 12). Using a different color for each sum, color the flower petals.

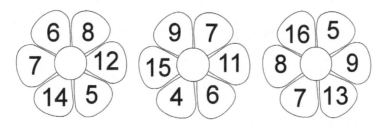

3. Marsha picked 12 oranges, 13 peaches, and 10 plums. Bonnie picked 8 oranges, 11 peaches, and 15 plums. Find the totals for each fruit. Then draw the bars for the bar graph.

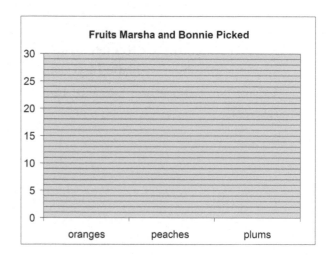

Skills Review 30

1. Don't write the answers; just practice the sums in your head.

$7 + 0 = \square$	$7 + 5 = \square$	$7 + 6 = \square$	$7 + 9 = \square$
$7 + 3 = \square$	$7 + 9 = \square$	$7 + 7 = \square$	$7 + 4 = \square$
$7 + 10 = \square$	$7 + 8 = \square$	$7 + 1 = \square$	$7 + 2 = \square$

2. Kyle and Alex have 11 toy cars in total that they share in various ways. The chart shows how many cars Kyle has in each case. Write how many Alex has. (The first one is done for you.)

Kyle	3	9	7	5	8	4	6
Alex	8						

3. Subtract.

a. $14 - 6 = $ _____	**b.** $17 - 8 = $ _____	**c.** $12 - 5 = $ _____

4. Let's say it is Wednesday. What day of the week will it be...

   a. in 3 days? _____ **b.** in 6 days? _____

5. Solve the word problems.

   a. Fifty-seven ants were marching across the yard.
   Twelve ants stopped to check out a bread crumb.
   Then twenty more stopped to crawl around on a
   leaf. How many ants were still marching across
   the yard?

   b. Mr. Phillips has 28 students in his class.
   One day, half of them arrived late.
   How many didn't arrive late?

Skills Review 31

Chapter 3

1. Write or say the time using the expressions *o'clock* or *half past*.

a. _____

b. _____

c. _____

d. _____

_____

_____

_____

_____

2. Add in your head. Color if the answer is 12.

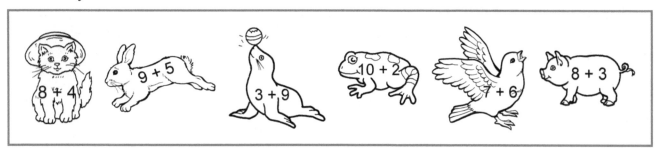

3. Complete these boxes!

Add 6 each time.
Add 7 each time.
Add 8 each time.

+ 6

4	10
7	___
8	___
10	___

+ 7

3	___
6	___
5	___
7	___

+ 8

2	___
4	___
7	___
8	___

4. Complete the next ten.

a. 72 + ____ = _____

b. 94 + ____ = _____

c. 51 + ____ = _____

Skills Review 32

1. Skip-count.

a. 12, 17, _____, _____, _____, _____, _____, _____, _____

b. 75, 73, _____, _____, _____, _____, _____, _____, _____

2. Sharon has a dentist appointment on the third Thursday in October. What date is Sharon's appointment?

_____

Four days after her dentist appointment, Sharon is going to go skiing in the mountains. What date is Sharon going to go skiing?

_____

October						
Su	Mo	Tu	We	Th	Fr	Sa
						1
2	3	4	5	6	7	8
9	10	11	12	13	14	15
16	17	18	19	20	21	22
23	24	25	26	27	28	29
30	31					

3. Add or subtract.

a.	b.	c.
43 + _____ = 93	31 + 40 = _____	_____ − 30 = 55

4. Solve the word problems.

a. Marissa has 7 cats, 15 goldfish, and 3 dogs. How many pets does Marissa have?

Marissa gave 6 of her goldfish to a friend. How many pets does Marissa have now?

b. Farmer Jones has 14 cows and Farmer Green has two times as many cows as Farmer Jones. How many cows does Farmer Green have?

1. Starting at the top, find the **odd** numbers and color a path through the maze.

7	12	2	10	4
16	19	10	14	6
8	11	18	22	16
13	28	20	18	4
10	25	16	12	24
22	31	50	30	32
36	24	39	36	28
42	46	43	40	46
72	41	46	48	42
53	50	48	56	54

2. Find the missing numbers.

a. $6 + \boxed{} = 14$

b. $\boxed{} - 8 = 5$

c. $13 - \boxed{} = 9$

d. $9 + \boxed{} = 14$

e. $\boxed{} + 7 = 14$

3. Solve these subtractions by thinking of the DISTANCE between two numbers.

a. $20 - 17 = $ _____	b. $97 - 92 = $ _____	c. $67 - 65 = $ _____

4. Solve the word problems.

a. On a nature hike, Mariah collected 9 rocks, 9 flowers, and 2 pine cones. Aaron collected 8 pine cones, 4 rocks, and 7 feathers.

Who collected more items? How many more?

b. Jim started putting a puzzle together at 2:30 and finished at 5:00. How long did it take him to put together the puzzle?

An hour and a half later, Jim had pizza for supper. What time did Jim eat supper?

Skills Review 34

1. Fill and color the number rainbow. Then practice the subtraction problems.

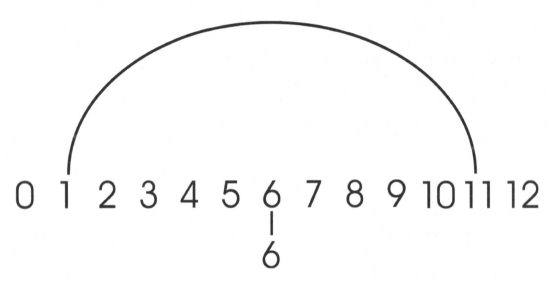

$12 - 8 =$ ▢ $12 - 3 =$ ▢ $12 - 4 =$ ▢ $12 - 9 =$ ▢

$12 - 6 =$ ▢ $12 - 10 =$ ▢ $12 - 7 =$ ▢ $12 - 5 =$ ▢

2. Add 8 to each number on the bottom. Notice the pattern!

6	12	18	24	30	36	42	48	54	60	66

3. Write the time using the expressions "past" or "till."

  a. 8:35 _____

  b. 11:20 _____

4. First, subtract to the previous whole ten. Then, subtract some more.

a. 61 − 8	**b.** 43 − 7	**c.** 82 − 9
/ \	/ \	/ \
61 − ___ − ___ = ___	43 − ___ − ___ = ___	82 − ___ − ___ = ___

Skills Review 35

1. Find the missing numbers.

a.	$7 + \underline{\hspace{2cm}} = 10$
b.	$44 + \underline{\hspace{2cm}} = 50$
c.	$12 + \underline{\hspace{2cm}} = 20$
d.	$33 + \underline{\hspace{2cm}} = 40$

2. Find one-half of the given numbers.

$\frac{1}{2}$ of 24 is _____.

$\frac{1}{2}$ of 18 is _____.

$\frac{1}{2}$ of 14 is _____.

$\frac{1}{2}$ of 30 is _____.

$\frac{1}{2}$ of 32 is _____.

3. Solve the puzzle to find out what Laura got for her birthday.

$9+4$	$15-7$	$6+9$	$8+8$	$14-6$	$5+7$	$8+9$

___ ___ ___ ___ ___ ___

$13-6$	$17-8$	$7+7$	$14-3$	$6+8$	$6+6$	$7+10$

___ ___ ___ ___ ___ ___ ___

Key:

L	P	I	R	C	Y	U	A	E	B
12	8	9	16	14	11	15	13	17	7

4. Solve the word problems.

a. At 7:00, Bruce started painting the shed.
It took him six hours to paint it.
What time did he finish?

b. Gwen had $57. Then, she bought a doll
for $14 and a sticker book for $4.
How much money does she have left?

Skills Review 36

1. Complete the next ten.

a. $73 +$ _____ $=$ _____	**b.** $41 +$ _____ $=$ _____	**c.** $95 +$ _____ $=$ _____

2. Subtract.

a. $15 - 6 =$ _____	**b.** $17 - 9 =$ _____	**c.** $16 - 7 =$ _____
d. $18 - 9 =$ _____	**e.** $15 - 7 =$ _____	**f.** $17 - 8 =$ _____

3. Harmony peeled 19 potatoes to make a big pot of potato soup and thought she was finished, but then her mom brought in 8 more potatoes that had been "hiding" in the back of the fridge. How many potatoes did she have to peel, in total?

4. **a.** Skippy Squirrel buried 33 acorns in the woods and Squeaky Squirrel buried 29. How many more acorns did Skippy Squirrel bury than Squeaky Squirrel?

   b. Uh oh! Squeaky Squirrel can only remember where he buried 19 of his acorns. How many of his acorns did he lose?

5. Put the letters in order to make a word. The first letter of your new word is "C."

B	E	O	A	C	I	T	L	N	R	E
5th	2nd	10th	7th	1st	9th	8th	3rd	11th	6th	4th

___ ___ ___ ___ ___ ___ ___ ___ ___ ___ ___

6. Fill in the missing dates in the table. Use the calendar to help!

Date 2 weeks ago	Date now	Date 2 weeks later
	November 23rd	

Skills Review 37

1. If the number is even, color the car blue. If the number is odd, color the car red.

2. Justin built a tower using 87 building blocks.
   Oh no! Justin's pet goat, Peter, came and licked
   the tower, and 30 of the blocks fell down.
   How many blocks are still standing?

3. Write the time that the clock shows,
   and the time 10 minutes later.

	a.	b.
	_____ : _____	_____ : _____
10 min. later →	_____ : _____	_____ : _____

4. Add or subtract.

a. $5 +$ _____ $= 11$

   $8 +$ _____ $= 12$

b. _____ $+ 3 = 12$

   _____ $+ 7 = 11$

c. $12 -$ _____ $= 5$

   $11 -$ _____ $= 2$

5. Draw the lines to show the additions on the number line.

a. $17 + 9 =$ _____

b. $16 + 15 =$ _____

Skills Review 38

1. Add. Compare the problems.

a. 9 + 7 = _____

   69 + 7 = _____

b. 9 + 4 = _____

   49 + 4 = _____

2. Write the time an hour later, and then another half-hour later. Use numbers.

Now it is:	**a.** 12:30	**b.** 4:00
An hour later, it is:		
Plus a half-hour later, it is:		

3. Write < , > , or = .

a. 74 + 7 ☐ 74 + 9   **b.** 30 − 5 ☐ 30 − 8   **c.** $\frac{1}{2}$ of 18 ☐ 9

4. **a.** Caleb had too many hats! He gave half of his hats to his friend Corey, and then he had 15 hats left. How many hats did Caleb have originally?

   b. Caleb still had too many hats! He gave 6 hats to the mailman. How many hats does Caleb have now?

5. Add in your head and color if the sum equals the number in the middle of the flower.

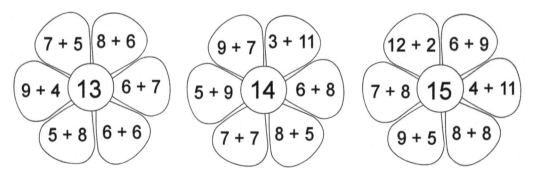

6. Find the differences.

a. The difference between 70 and 67	**b.** The difference between 100 and 96

Skills Review 39

1. Let's say it is March now. How many months is it...

   ...until July? _____   ...until October? _____   ...until December? _____

2. Add.

a. $17 + 9 =$ _____	b. $36 + 5 =$ _____	c. $78 + 7 =$ _____

3. Find the pattern and continue it.

$64 - 10 =$ _____

$64 - 20 =$ _____

$64 -$ ___ $=$ _____

$64 -$ ___ $=$ _____

$64 -$ ___ $=$ _____

$64 -$ ___ $=$ _____

4. Add or subtract.

a. $17 - 8 =$ _____
b. $9 +$ _____ $= 18$
c. _____ $- 7 = 8$
d. $6 + 11 =$ _____
e. $14 -$ _____ $= 5$
f. $7 +$ _____ $= 16$

5. Solve the word problems.

a. On Friday, Daren ordered a book online and it arrived five days later. What day of the week did it arrive?

b. Grace got up at 8:00 this morning. What time did she go to sleep if she slept 9 hours?

Tomorrow morning, Grace has to get up two hours earlier than she did today. What time will that be?

Skills Review 40

1. Fill in and color the number rainbow. Then practice the subtractions.

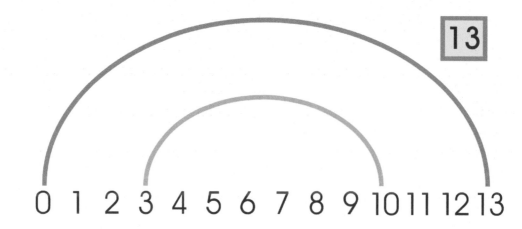

13 – 7 = ▢   13 – 4 = ▢   13 – 9 = ▢   13 – 10 = ▢

13 – 5 = ▢   13 – 6 = ▢   13 – 11 = ▢   13 – 8 = ▢

2. How many hours is it?

from	12 midnight	5 AM
to	12 noon	3 PM
hours		

3. Divide these shapes into two halves. Then color one half.

a.   b.   c.

4. Add. Regroup if you can make a new ten from the ones.

a.   3 6   b.   4 3   c.   5 7   d.   7 9   e.   6 4
   + 1 5   + 4 5   + 2 8   + 1 6   + 2 6

5. Solve the problem. Write a number sentence, not just the answer.

> Seth had $28. Then the neighbor paid him $7 for walking the dog. How much money does he have now?

Skills Review 41

1. Fill in the missing dates in the table. Use the calendar to help!

Date 1 week ago	Date now	Date 1 week later
	August 26th	

2. Add.

a.
```
    4 7
    2 5
+   1 4
_____
```

b.
```
    7 2
      8
+   3 6
_____
```

c.
```
    5 3
    7 9
+   3 4
_____
```

d.
```
    1 5
    6 9
+   7 3
_____
```

e.
```
    9 0
+   6 8
      7
_____
```

3. Figure out the pattern and continue it!

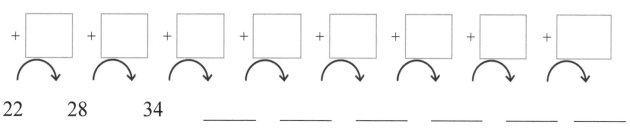

22   28   34   ____ ____ ____ ____ ____ ____

4. Subtract.

a. $33 - 9 =$ _____	b. $61 - 6 =$ _____	c. $75 - 8 =$ _____

5. Solve the word problems. Write number sentences, not just the answers.

a. Joy has 17 tomato plants, 30 green bean plants, and 6 pepper plants in her garden. How many plants does she have in total?

b. A very hungry grasshopper came along and ate 5 of her plants! How many plants does she have left?

Skills Review 42

1. Add.

a.	b.	c.	d.	e.
3 9	5 3	2 4	7 2	6 6
+ 1 7	+ 4 5	+ 5 6	+ 2 7	+ 1 8

2. Fill in the missing numbers.

a. $18 - \bigcirc = 9$ b. $\bigcirc - 9 = 8$ c. $\bigcirc - 7 = 9$

3. Amy and Kim have 14 figurines together.

   a. Complete the chart below so that it shows different ways they could share those figurines.

   b. Circle all the odd numbers in the chart.

Amy							
Kim	10	5	11	8	6	9	7

4. Add *in parts*. Break the number that is not whole tens into its tens and ones in your mind.

a. $14 + 10 = $ _____	b. $26 + 20 = $ _____	c. $40 + 18 = $ _____

5. Write the time that the clock shows, and the time 5 minutes later.

	a. 	b. 	c. 	d. 
	_____ : _____	_____ : _____	_____ : _____	_____ : _____
5 min. later →	_____ : _____	_____ : _____	_____ : _____	_____ : _____

Skills Review 43

1. Solve the subtractions by thinking of the <u>distance between the numbers</u>—how far apart they are from each other.

a.	b.	c.	d.
$73 - 67 = $ _____	$60 - 55 = $ _____	$32 - 29 = $ _____	$84 - 82 = $ _____

2. Melody found 7 crayons under her bed, 9 crayons in her closet, and 4 crayons in a sock. She shared them equally with her sister Harmony. How many crayons did each girl get?

3. Write $<$, $>$, or $=$.

   a. $39 + 5$ ☐ $37 + 7$ b. $40 - 9$ ☐ $45 - 9$ c. 69 ☐ $76 - 9$

4. Add four numbers in pairs.

a. $9 + 7 + 6 + 8$	b. $4 + 8 + 7 + 3$	c. $5 + 9 + 4 + 9$
= _____ + _____ = _____	= _____ + _____ = _____	= _____ + _____ = _____

5. Write the time using the expressions "past," "till," or "half past."

   a. 1:30 _____

   b. 7:45 _____

   c. 3:20 _____

6. Add.

a. $29 + 5 = $ _____	b. $69 + 3 = $ _____	c. $99 + 4 = $ _____

Skills Review 44

1. Write the numbers so that the ones and tens are in their own columns. Add.

    a. $42 + 6 + 14$ **b.** $9 + 23 + 4$ **c.** $54 + 12 + 5$ **d.** $7 + 8 + 36$ **e.** $18 + 3 + 48$

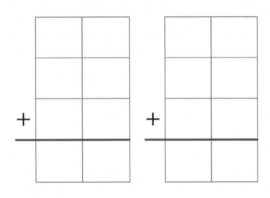
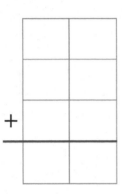
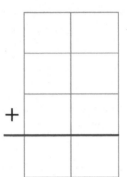

2. Starting at the top, find your way through the maze by coloring the number that is **one half** of the previous number.

50	32	48	26	18
14	24	21	15	20
8	11	12	22	16
13	5	20	6	4
9	25	3	4	24

3. Complete the next ten.

    a. $51 + \underline{\quad} = \underline{\qquad}$

    b. $63 + \underline{\quad} = \underline{\qquad}$

    c. $44 + \underline{\quad} = \underline{\qquad}$

    d. $92 + \underline{\quad} = \underline{\qquad}$

4. Cheryl and Gavin played a game. Cheryl got 47 points and Gavin got 39 points. How many more points did Cheryl get than Gavin?

5. Add or subtract.

a. $\underline{\quad} - 7 = 5$	**b.** $7 + \underline{\quad} = 11$	**c.** $12 - 9 = \underline{\quad}$
d. $8 + \underline{\quad} = 12$	**e.** $11 - \underline{\quad} = 6$	**f.** $6 + \underline{\quad} = 12$

Skills Review 45

1. Which animal is…

   a. …second from the right? _____ **b.** …fourth from the left? _____

   c. …eighth from the left? _____ **d.** …third from the right? _____

2. Add or subtract.

a. $28 + 6 =$ _____	**b.** $15 - 6 =$ _____	**c.** $48 + 7 =$ _____
d. $24 - 7 =$ _____	**e.** $68 + 9 =$ _____	**f.** $36 - 9 =$ _____

3. Write the time using the expressions
   o'clock or *half past.*

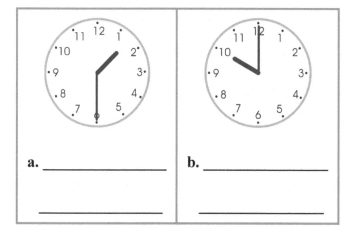

   a. _____

   _____

   b. _____

   _____

4. Find the pattern and continue it.

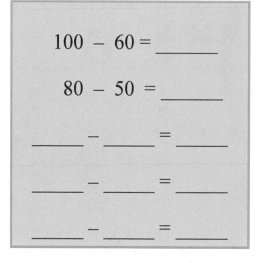

$100 - 60 =$ _____

$80 - 50 =$ _____

_____ $-$ _____ $=$ _____

_____ $-$ _____ $=$ _____

_____ $-$ _____ $=$ _____

5. Solve the problem. Write a number sentence, not just the answer.

Craig's grandpa has a small orchard. In that
orchard, he has eight apple trees, five cherry
trees, three plum trees, and six peach trees.
How many fruit trees does Craig's grandpa
have in his orchard, in total?

Skills Review 46

1. Fill in and color the number rainbow. Then practice the subtractions.

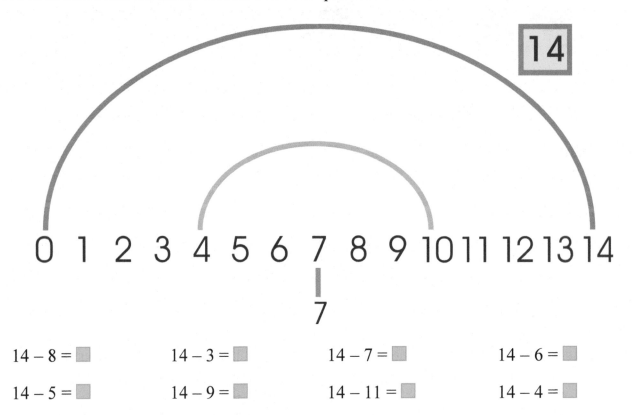

$$14 - 8 = \square \qquad 14 - 3 = \square \qquad 14 - 7 = \square \qquad 14 - 6 = \square$$

$$14 - 5 = \square \qquad 14 - 9 = \square \qquad 14 - 11 = \square \qquad 14 - 4 = \square$$

2. Find the hidden shapes in this picture. Color the quadrilaterals blue, the triangle green, the hexagon red, and the pentagons yellow.

3. Maya started doing her homework at 2:00 and finished at 5:00. How long did it take Maya to do her homework?

4. Figure out the missing numbers for these addition problems.

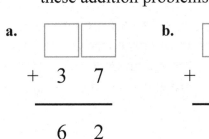

a.
$$\begin{array}{r} \square\square \\ +\ 3\ 7 \\ \hline 6\ 2 \end{array}$$

b.
$$\begin{array}{r} \square\square \\ +\ \ \ 5 \\ \hline 9\ 3 \end{array}$$

Skills Review 47

1. Add.

a.
```
   1 6
 + 5 8
 _____
```

b.
```
   3 9
   2 7
 + 1 2
 _____
```

c.
```
   4 0
   1 7
 + 3 4
 _____
```

d.
```
   2 6
   3 8
 + 2 5
 _____
```

e.
```
   5 4
 + 1 9
 _____
```

2. Draw rectangles so they have the given number of little squares inside. Guess and check!

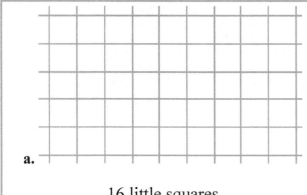

a.

16 little squares

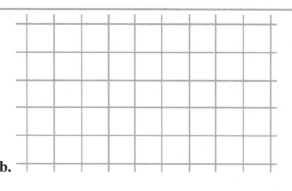

b.

20 little squares

3. Let's review some doubles!

7 + 7 = _____	32 + 32 = _____
8 + 8 = _____	45 + 45 = _____
9 + 9 = _____	60 + 60 = _____

4. Find the missing numbers.

a. $9 + \boxed{} = 13$

b. $13 - \boxed{} = 7$

c. $\boxed{} + 8 = 13$

5. Solve the word problems.

a. Today is Tuesday. Jason went to a water park 8 days ago. On what day of the week did he go to the water park?

b. A red dress costs $39, and a blue dress costs $45. What is the difference in price of the two dresses?

Skills Review 48

1. Add mentally.

a. 27 + 43 = _____	**b.** 13 + 16 = _____
c. 8 + 30 + 5 + 7 = _____	**d.** 40 + 20 + 6 + 4 = _____

2. Think of the ANSWERS.
   Then match:

     7 + 7   9 + 6

              EVEN

     5 + 6   8 + 5

     7 + 8   7 + 4

              ODD

     6 + 7   6 + 8

3. Practice making this shape using
   your cutout shapes.

4. Show the addition on the number line.

16 + 9 + 5 = _____

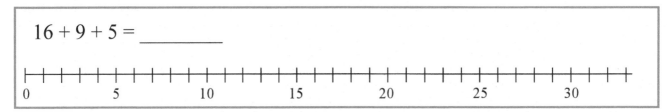

5. Write < , > , or = .

a. 74 − 7 ☐ 63 + 8   **b.** 36 + 8 ☐ 53 − 9   **c.** 82 − 4 ☐ 69 + 8

6. Solve the problems.

a. It is 10:00 and Alex has been working in the barn for three hours. What time did Alex start working?
b. Farmer Joe had 49 sheep. Then, he sold 20 of them. The next day, 6 lambs were born. How many sheep does Farmer Joe have now?

Skills Review 49

1. Continue the pattern.

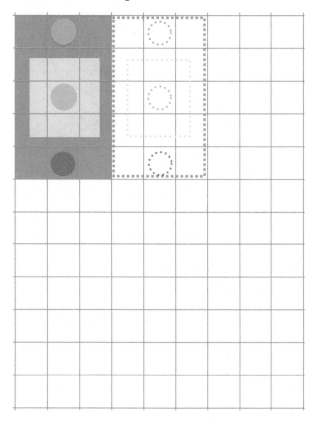

2. Add.

a. $29 + 5 =$ _____
b. $59 + 7 =$ _____
c. $79 + 4 =$ _____

3. Subtract.

a. $15 - 8 =$ _____
b. $16 - 9 =$ _____
c. $15 - 10 =$ _____
d. $16 - 7 =$ _____

4. October 13th is Dustin's birthday. His cousin
   Reuben's birthday is two weeks earlier.
   When is Reuben's birthday?

5. Write the time.

a. _____ : _____   b. _____ : _____   c. _____ : _____   d. _____ : _____

6. Fill in the missing numbers.

a. $76 -$ _____ $= 36$	b. $42 +$ _____ $= 92$	c. $88 -$ _____ $= 58$

Skills Review 50

1. Find the total cost.

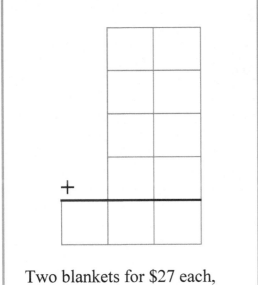

Two blankets for $27 each,
two lamps for $49 each.

2. Subtract.

a. 43 − 9 = _____	
b. 65 − 7 = _____	
c. 88 − 6 = _____	
d. 52 − 8 = _____	
e. 91 − 5 = _____	
f. 34 − 7 = _____	

3. Seventeen elephants were rolling in the mud. Then twenty more elephants came along and joined them.

   a. How many elephants are rolling in the mud now?

   b. Eight of the elephants decided to go rest in the shade. How many elephants are rolling in the mud now?

4. Label the pictures with *box, cube, cylinder, pyramid,* or *cone.*

   a.      **b.**   **c.**

_____   _____   _____

5. Add 5 to each number on the bottom. Notice the pattern!

11									
6	12	18	24	30	36	42	48	54	60

Skills Review 51

1. Fill in the missing numbers.

a. $14 - 6 =$ _____	**b.** $9 +$ _____ $= 15$	**c.** _____ $- 9 = 5$
d. _____ $- 9 = 9$	**e.** _____ $- 7 = 10$	**f.** _____ $+ 8 = 15$

2. Write the time using the words "past" or "till", and using numbers.

3. Match.

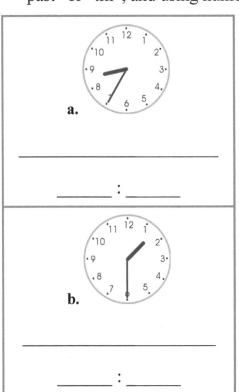

a.

_____

_____ : _____

b.

_____

_____ : _____

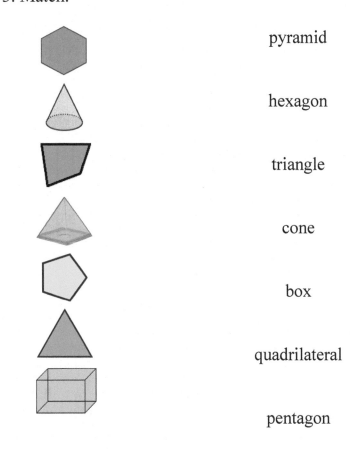

pyramid

hexagon

triangle

cone

box

quadrilateral

pentagon

4. Write a "*how many more*" addition to find the difference between the numbers.

a. The difference between 27 and 19
_____ $+$ _____ $=$ _____
b. The difference between 6 and 13
_____ $+$ _____ $=$ _____

5. Divide these shapes. Then color as you are asked to.

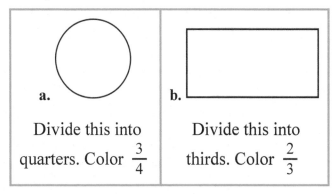

a.

Divide this into quarters. Color $\frac{3}{4}$

b.

Divide this into thirds. Color $\frac{2}{3}$

Skills Review 52

1. How many hours is it?

from	12 midnight	3 AM	8 AM	10 AM	6 AM
to	12 noon	7 PM	2 PM	5 PM	11 PM
hours					

2. Write the previous and next **whole ten**. Then, circle the ten that is nearer the given number.

a. _____, 47, _____

b. _____, 83, _____

c. _____, 66, _____

3. Continue the pattern.

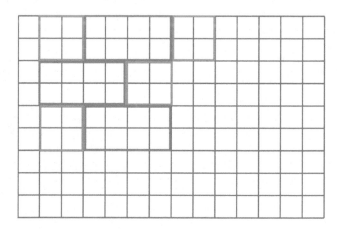

4. Solve the word problems by adding or subtracting in columns.

a. Allison played with her jump rope for 25 minutes.
Peter played with his jump rope for 37 minutes.
How much longer did Peter jump rope than Allison?

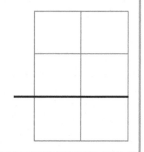

b. Mia dug up 28 potatoes and Cheryl dug up 19.
How many potatoes did the two girls dig up, in total?

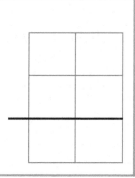

Skills Review 53

1. Practice making this shape with your cut-outs.

2. Add or subtract.

a. $68 + 6 =$ _____
b. $50 - 9 =$ _____
c. $73 + 7 =$ _____
d. $20 - 3 =$ _____
e. $35 + 8 =$ _____

3. Meredith cleaned under her bed. She found nine socks, six crayons, eight peanuts, and seven newborn kittens (Surprise!). How many things did Meredith find under her bed?

4. Joel started studying for his English test at 2:30 and finished an hour and a half later. What time did he finish?

5. Write each number as a double of some other number.

a. $16 =$ ____ + ____	**b.** $80 =$ ____ + ____	**c.** $30 =$ ____ + ____

6. Divide the shapes into two, three, or four equal parts so that you can color the fraction. Then compare and write $<$, $>$, or $=$.

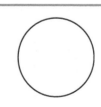

a.
$\frac{2}{3}$ $\frac{1}{2}$

b.
$\frac{2}{3}$ $\frac{3}{4}$

Skills Review 54

1. Write the time that the clock shows, and the time 5 minutes later.

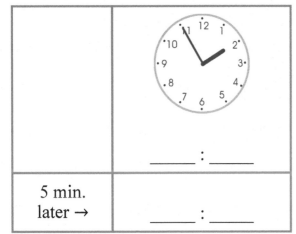

	____ : ____
5 min. later →	____ : ____

2. Write a sum of the hundreds, tens, and ones shown in the picture. Also write the number.

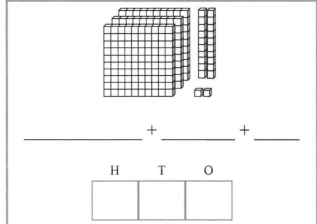

_____ + _____ + _____

H	T	O

3. Add.

a.
```
    5 6
    3 9
+ 7 6
```

b.
```
    2 3
    4 2
+ 9 5
```

c.
```
    1 8
    5 4
+ 1 9
```

d.
```
    4 5
    8 1
+ 7 9
```

e.
```
    2 7
    4 9
+ 7 6
```

4. Use letters from the given word to make a new word.

W A T E R M E L O N

____ ____ ____ ____ ____
1st   9th   6th   2nd   10th

5. Practice mental subtraction. Don't write the answers; just think them in your head.

$14 - 7 =$ ▨ $12 - 5 =$ ▨ $11 - 8 =$ ▨

$14 - 5 =$ ▨ $12 - 9 =$ ▨ $11 - 4 =$ ▨

$14 - 3 =$ ▨ $12 - 6 =$ ▨ $11 - 2 =$ ▨

$14 - 9 =$ ▨ $12 - 8 =$ ▨ $11 - 5 =$ ▨

6. Add 8 to each number on the bottom.

9	18	27	36	45	54	63	72	81	90	99	108

Skills Review 55

1. Let's say it is Tuesday. What day of the week will it be...

   a. in 3 days? _____ **b.** in 8 days? _____

2. Label the pictures as *box*, *cylinder*, *pyramid*, or *cone*.

   a.   **b.**   **c.**

   _____   _____   _____

3. Mark on the number line: 279, 241, 302, 257, 227, 308, 293, 234, 216, 268.

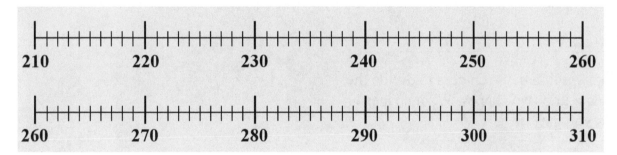

4. Divide the numbers into two EQUAL parts. Write an addition. Find half of the total.

a. 22	**b.** 50	**c.** 44
____ + ____ = ____	____ + ____ = ____	____ + ____ = ____
$\frac{1}{2}$ of 22 is ____	$\frac{1}{2}$ of 50 is ____	$\frac{1}{2}$ of 44 is ____

5. Solve the word problems.

a. Last year Mrs. Harrison had 12 boys and 13 girls in her class. This year she has 4 more boys and 2 more girls. How many students does she have this year?
b. Robert is 47 years old and Michael is 52. What is the difference between the two men's ages?

Skills Review 56

1. Add.

| **a.** $69 + 5 =$ _____ | **b.** $17 + 9 =$ _____ | **c.** $36 + 6 =$ _____ |

2. At 2:35, Brett started bathing his dog, Pickles. Five minutes later, Pickles ran away and Brett had to chase her for ten minutes before he caught her! What time was it when Brett caught Pickles?

3. Connect the dots. Use a ruler! What shape do you get?

   _____

4. Draw a line between dots to divide the shape into two shapes. What shapes do you get?

   _____

   _____

5. Find the pattern and complete it.

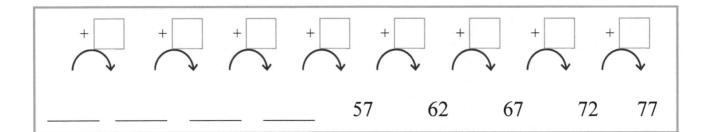

_____   _____   _____   _____   57   62   67   72   77

6. Tell what fraction is colored.

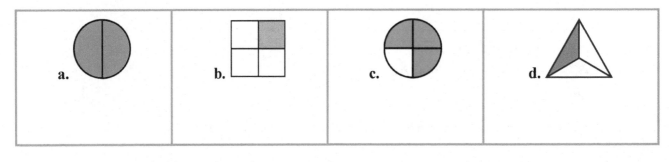

a.   **b.**   **c.**   **d.**

1. Compare. Write $<$, $>$, or $=$ in the box.

| **a.** $66 + 5$ ☐ $77 - 8$ | **b.** $81 - 6$ ☐ $69 + 6$ | **c.** $43 - 4$ ☐ $34 + 7$ |

2. Add or subtract.

a. $563 + 300 =$ _____

b. $741 - 500 =$ _____

c. $876 - 400 =$ _____

3. Add mentally and color.

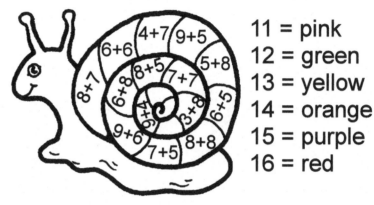

11 = pink
12 = green
13 = yellow
14 = orange
15 = purple
16 = red

4. Write either $<$ or $>$ in between the numbers.

| **a.** 356   342 | **b.** 102   112 | **c.** 517   506 | **d.** 741   752 |

5. One of the "parts" for the numbers is missing. Find what it is.

a. $200 +$ △ $+ 7 = 257$

△ $=$ _____

b. △ $+ 800 + 3 = 893$

△ $=$ _____

c. $6 +$ △ $+ 40 = 746$

△ $=$ _____

6. Solve the problems.

a. Becky took a painting class that started in June and lasted for seven months. What month was the last month of the class?

b. Dad found eight crackers in the cupboard and twelve crackers on the washing machine. He shared them equally with Sandra. How many crackers did each one get?

Skills Review 58

1. Angela plans to go hiking every Friday during the month of November. What dates will she go hiking?

   November _____   November _____

   November _____   November _____

November						
Su	Mo	Tu	We	Th	Fr	Sa
		1	2	3	4	5
6	7	8	9	10	11	12
13	14	15	16	17	18	19
20	21	22	23	24	25	26
27	28	29	30			

2. Figure out the missing numbers.

a. ☐☐
    + 1 4
    ———
    7 3

b. ☐☐
    + 3
    ———
    5 5

c. ☐☐
    + 2 5
    ———
    8 2

d. ☐☐
    + 3 8
    ———
    6 4

e. ☐☐
    + 1 9
    ———
    4 8

3. How many hours does Kayla work if she starts and stops at the given times?

Start work	9 AM	7 AM
End work	5 PM	6 PM
Work hours		

4. Divide this shape into two shapes so that you get a quadrilateral and a triangle.

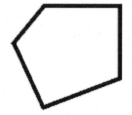

5. Subtract.

a. $31 - 27 =$ _____	b. $50 - 45 =$ _____	c. $23 - 17 =$ _____	d. $42 - 35 =$ _____

6. Fill in the addition table.

+	6	8	4	5	7	3	9
6							
7							
8							

Skills Review 59

1. Write the number that is 10 less and 10 more than the given number.

   a. _____, 725, _____   b. _____, 203, _____

2. Continue the pattern.

3. Subtract.

a. $27 + 2 =$ _____

$27 + 4 =$ _____

$27 +$ ___ $=$ _____

$27 +$ ___ $=$ _____

$27 +$ ___ $=$ _____

a. $680 - 200 =$ _____

b. $274 - 50 =$ _____

c. $736 - 400 =$ _____

d. $98 - 30 =$ _____

4. Write the time using the expressions "past," "till," or "half past."

   a. 1:15 _____

   b. 5:30 _____

   c. 11:35 _____

5. Find the total cost.

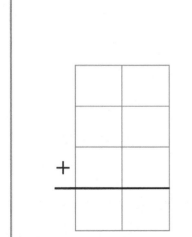

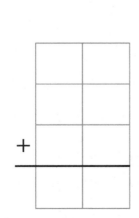

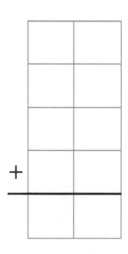

a. Two games at $19 each; a dress for $27.

b. Three dolls for $15 each.

c. Two vases for $14 each; two paintings for $32 each.

Skills Review 60

1. Write or say the time using the expressions *o'clock* or *half past*.

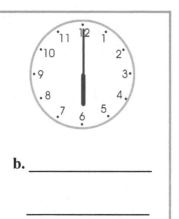

a. _____

_____

b. _____

_____

2. Complete the next hundred.

a. 60 + _____ = _____

b. 120 + _____ = _____

c. 580 + _____ = _____

d. 740 + _____ = _____

3. Damon has 480 stamps in his collection and Paula has 300. How many more stamps does Damon have than Paula?

4. Subtract.

a. $41 - 6 =$ _____   b. $55 - 8 =$ _____   c. $23 - 5 =$ _____

5. Compare the expressions and write $<$, $>$, or $=$.

a. $6 + 9 + 5$ ☐ $7 + 6 + 8$ b. $4 + 7 + 9$ ☐ $8 + 6 + 4$

6. Draw rectangles so they have the given number of little squares inside. Guess and check!

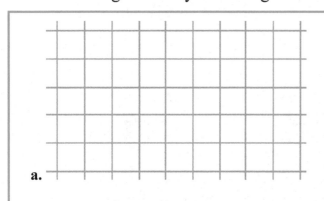

a.

18 little squares

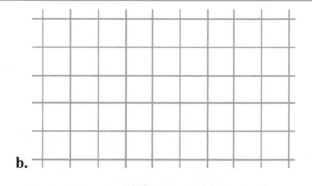

b.

24 little squares

Skills Review 61

1. Find the missing numbers.

a. $11 - \underline{\quad} = 5$	**b.** $\underline{\quad} + 7 = 12$	**c.** $13 - 6 = \underline{\quad}$
d. $7 + \underline{\quad} = 14$	**e.** $14 - \underline{\quad} = 9$	**f.** $\underline{\quad} + 4 = 11$

2. Color. Then compare and write < , > , or = . Which is more "pie" to eat?

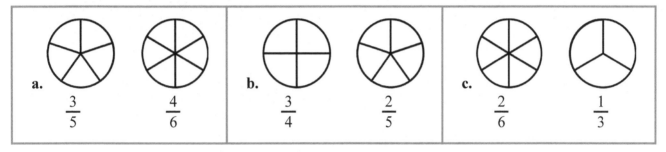

a. $\dfrac{3}{5}$ $\dfrac{4}{6}$	**b.** $\dfrac{3}{4}$ $\dfrac{2}{5}$	**c.** $\dfrac{2}{6}$ $\dfrac{1}{3}$

3. Write the later time.

Time now	1:25
5 min. later	___ : ___

Time now	7:55
10 min. later	___ : ___

4. Subtract.

a. $1000 - 700 = \underline{\quad\quad}$
b. $1000 - 300 - 500 = \underline{\quad\quad}$
c. $1000 - 400 = \underline{\quad\quad}$

5. Sharon had $78. Then, she bought a puppy for $50 and a bag of puppy chow for $12. How much money does Sharon have now?

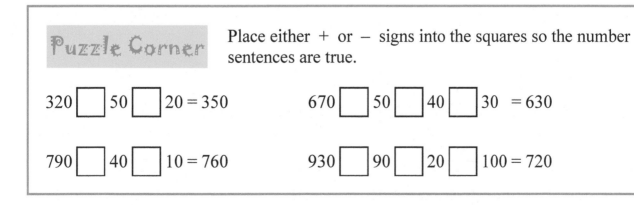

Puzzle Corner

Place either + or − signs into the squares so the number sentences are true.

$320 \;\square\; 50 \;\square\; 20 = 350$ $670 \;\square\; 50 \;\square\; 40 \;\square\; 30 = 630$

$790 \;\square\; 40 \;\square\; 10 = 760$ $930 \;\square\; 90 \;\square\; 20 \;\square\; 100 = 720$

Skills Review 62

1. The graph shows how many people went to the library on different days.

   a. How many more people went to the library on Friday than Thursday?

   _____

   b. How many people went to the library on Monday and Tuesday, in total?

   _____

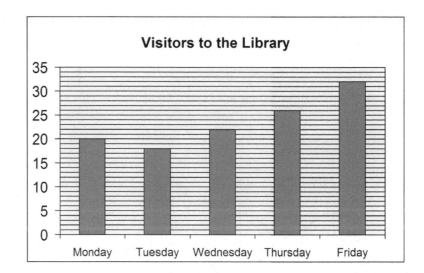

2. Write each number as a double of some other number.

a. 70 = ____ + ____	**b.** 58 = ____ + ____	**c.** 66 = ____ + ____

3. Add in columns.

a.	**b.**	**c.**	**d.**	**e.**
6 2	3 5	4 7	1 8	6 9
+ 9	4 4	+ 3 6	5 3	+ 1 3
	+ 1 6		+ 1 2	

4. Fill in the weekday before and after the given day.

	Saturday	

5. Solve the word problem.

Mom left 48 muffins on the counter to cool. Oh no! Sammy left the door open, and the chickens came into the house and gobbled up 25 muffins! How many muffins are left?

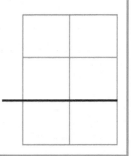

Skills Review 63

1. The pictograph shows how many cupcakes different girls baked for a school bake sale. Each cupcake picture means 4 cupcakes. One half of a cupcake would be half that.

a. Who baked the fewest cupcakes? _____

   How many did she bake? _____

b. How many more cupcakes did Kayla bake than Diana? _____

c. How many cupcakes did Melissa, Allison, and Shauna bake in total? _____

2. Find the missing numbers.

a. _____ − 70 = 340	
b. _____ − 30 = 760	
c. 895 − _____ = 835	
d. 249 − 50 = _____	

3. Practice making this shape with your cut-outs.

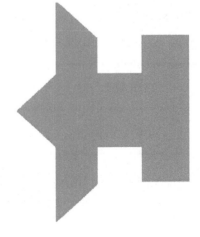

4. Add mentally.

a. 17 + 13 = _____	b. 15 + 20 = _____	c. 34 + 27 = _____

Skills Review 64

1. Write the time using the wordings "past" or "till", and using numbers.

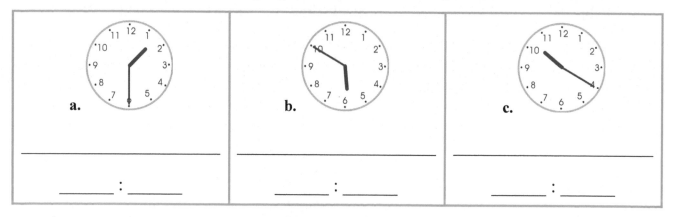

a. _____

_____ : _____

b. _____

_____ : _____

c. _____

_____ : _____

2. Add.

a.
```
    5 7
    1 8
  + 2 3
  _____
```

b.
```
    3 2
    2 9
  + 2 5
  _____
```

c.
```
    1 9
    2 7
  + 3 6
  _____
```

d.
```
    2 6
    3 5
  + 1 7
  _____
```

e.
```
    6 4
    1 3
  + 1 8
  _____
```

3. At your house, find the objects listed on the chart. First GUESS how long or tall they are. Then measure each object to the nearest centimeter and write "about" before the centimeter-amount, such as *about 8 cm*.

Item	GUESS	MEASUREMENT
coffee cup	cm	cm
toothbrush	cm	cm
nail clippers	cm	cm

4. Subtract or add whole hundreds many times.

a.	b.
$700 - 300 - 200 - 100 =$ _____	$400 + 200 + 100 + 300 =$ _____
$900 - 400 - 100 - 100 =$ _____	$200 + 200 + 300 + 100 =$ _____

Skills Review 65

1. Write the name of the shape. Then, measure to find the length of each side.

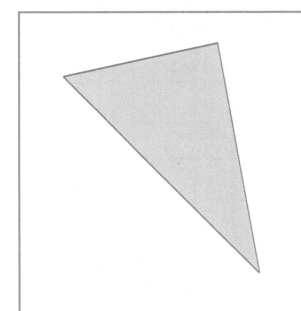

Side AB _____ inches

Side BC _____ inches

Side CA _____ inches

2. Add.

a. $17 + 9 =$ _____

b. $26 + 6 =$ _____

c. $49 + 8 =$ _____

3. Complete.

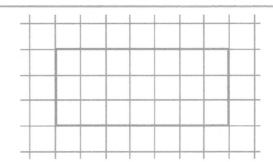

Divide this into thirds. Color $\frac{2}{3}$.

_____ little squares in two thirds

_____ little squares in the whole rectangle

4. Subtract. Think of the difference.

a. $33 - 27 =$ _____	b. $52 - 49 =$ _____	c. $74 - 68 =$ _____
d. $48 - 39 =$ _____	e. $21 - 16 =$ _____	f. $91 - 84 =$ _____

5. Write one half of each number.

22	26	30	34	38	42	46	50	54	58

1. Which unit would you use to find the following distances: inches (in), feet (ft), miles (mi), or feet and inches (ft in)?

Distance	Unit
from your wrist to your thumb	
from your house to the library	
the length of your bed	

2. How many hours is it?

from	7 AM	12 noon
to	9 PM	2 AM
hours		

3. **a.** The sixth shape from the right is a _____ .

   b. The first shape from the left is a _____ . It has _____ faces.

   c. The fourth shape from the right is a _____ . It has _____ faces.

   d. The ninth shape from the left is a _____ .

4. Solve the problems.

a. Twenty-six blackbirds, nine sparrows, and fourteen doves landed in a field. How many birds were there, in total?

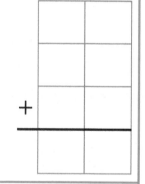

b. At a picnic, Beth and Joe were going to share 38 chocolate chips equally. Oops! They dropped 16 of them in the mud, so they threw them away. How many chocolate chips will each child get?

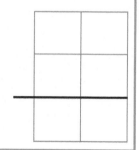

Skills Review 67

Chapter 7

1. Measure the fingers on both of your hands or the fingers of a friend, and make a line plot. On the line, write an "X" mark for the length each finger.

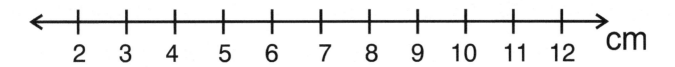

How much longer is your longest finger than your shortest finger?

2. Write either < or > in between the numbers.

| a. 236   310 | b. 127   122 | c. 574   569 | d. 736   754 |

3. Fill in the missing dates in the table. Use the calendar to help!

Date 2 weeks ago	Date now	Date 1 week later
	October 12	
	April 25	

4. Serena loves to collect stickers! Last week, she bought 8 stickers and yesterday, her mom gave her 20 for her birthday. Now she has 85 stickers. How many did she have originally?

5. Circle the odd numbers with a blue crayon and the even numbers with a red crayon.

| 102   293   719   348   186   337   195   152   544 |

Skills Review 68

1. Which unit would you use to find these below: centimeters (cm), meters (m), or kilometers (km)?

Distance	Unit
from your bedroom to the kitchen	
from Chicago to Miami	
the length of a nail	
the length of a sailboat	

2. Draw dots in the grid and join them so that you get a pentagon. Then draw a hexagon.

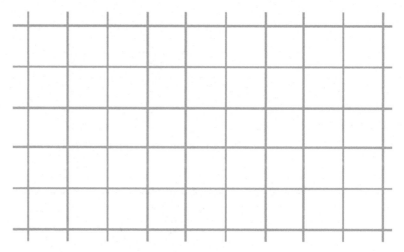

3. Find out what number the triangle represents.

a. $9 + \triangle + 30 = 639$

$\triangle = $ _____

b. $300 + 5 + \triangle = 385$

$\triangle = $ _____

4. Let's review some addition facts. Do not write the answers down. Just practice the sums.

6 + 4 = ☐	9 + 5 = ☐	7 + 8 = ☐	9 + 4 = ☐
8 + 3 = ☐	7 + 6 = ☐	9 + 9 = ☐	8 + 10 = ☐
9 + 7 = ☐	9 + 8 = ☐	6 + 5 = ☐	7 + 7 = ☐

5. Solve.

a. Starting at 11:00, Peyton worked on a craft project for two hours. What time did he finish?

b. Rhonda and Karly shared equally 800 beads. Then, Rhonda gave 200 of her beads to Kim. How many beads does Rhonda have now?

Skills Review 69

1. Write the numbers in the grids. Add.

   a. 8 + 12 + 34   **b.** 20 + 5 + 17   **c.** 41 + 9 + 43   **d.** 7 + 6 + 14

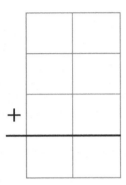 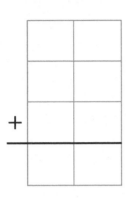 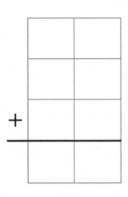 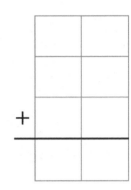

2. Fill in the missing numbers.

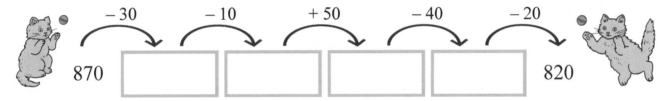

3. Weigh the following items. Write their weights below.

   A bag full of fruit (such as oranges or

   apples) _____ lb

   A big bowl of rocks _____ lb

   A big box of toys _____ lb

4. Let's say it is May now. What month will it be...

   a. in 2 months? _____

   b. in 7 months? _____

   c. in 4 months? _____

   d. in 9 months? _____

5. Color. Then compare and write < , > , or = . Which is more "pie" to eat?

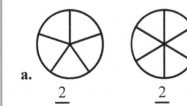 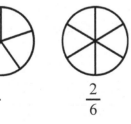 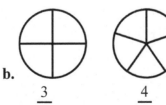 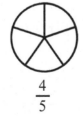

  a. $\frac{2}{5}$ $\frac{2}{6}$ **b.** $\frac{3}{4}$ $\frac{4}{5}$ **c.** $\frac{4}{6}$ $\frac{2}{3}$

Skills Review 70

1. The pictograph shows how many animals the Wilson family saw during a camping trip. Each animal picture means <u>three</u> animals. Draw a bar graph.

Animal	
Squirrels	
Rabbits	
Birds	
Fish	

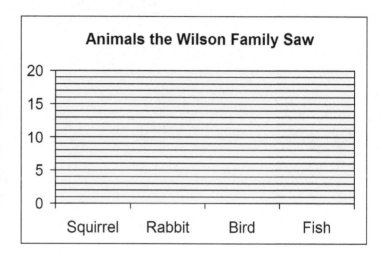

2. Add. You need to regroup ten tens as a new hundred.

a.
```
   9 0
 + 4 0
```

b.
```
   4 8 0
 +   6 0
```

c.
```
   7 2
 + 5 3
```

d.
```
   4 5 3
 +   5 4
```

e.
```
   6 3 6
 + 2 9 2
```

3. Find out how many kilograms three friends weigh. Write a list below.

_____ _____ kg

_____ _____ kg

_____ _____ kg

4. Farmer Green harvested some melons. He gave 20 to the Hill family and 13 to Mr. Smith, and now he has 30 left. How many melons did Farmer Green harvest?

5. Mark these numbers approximately on the number line: 893, 972, 998, 904, 965.

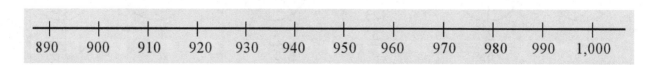

Skills Review 71

1. Rabbit is 12 centimeters away from a yummy carrot! Measure and mark where the carrot should be on the line, and draw it.

 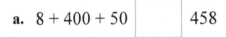

2. Add. Regroup two times if necessary.

a. 7 0 8 + 2 6 4	b. 2 8 7 + 2 3 9	c. 5 9 6 + 3 2 5	d. 2 7 8 + 4 3 6

3. Compare and write < , > , or = .

   a. 8 + 400 + 50 ☐ 458

   b. 200 + 4 + 30 ☐ 40 + 3 + 300

   c. 60 + 800 + 9 ☐ 90 + 700 + 5

4. Practice making this shape with your cut-outs.

5. Add or subtract.

a. 27 + 9 = _____	b. 45 − 8 = _____	c. 54 + 7 = _____

My ones digit is double my tens digit. The sum of my digits is 12.

Skills Review 72

1. Mark on the number line: 288, 297, 305, 301, 299, 226, 243, 268, 222, 309.

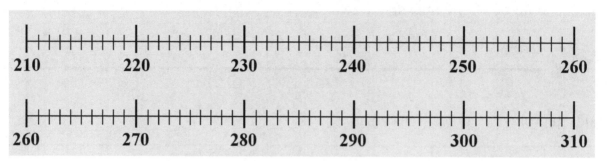

2. Add.

a.
```
    4 9
    2 7
    2 1
  + 1 5
  ──────
```

b.
```
    5 2
    2 8
  + 4 5
  ──────
```

c.
```
    1 1
    7 3
    5 4
  + 2 6
  ──────
```

d.
```
    2 2
    7 9
  + 1 4
  ──────
```

e.
```
    1 2
    8 1
    3 5
  + 1 6
  ──────
```

3. First GUESS how long these lines are in inches and half-inches. Write down your guess. After that, measure how long the lines are.

	GUESS	MEASUREMENT
a.	_____ inches	_____ inches
b.	_____ inches	_____ inches

4. Write the time using the wordings "past" or "till", and using numbers.

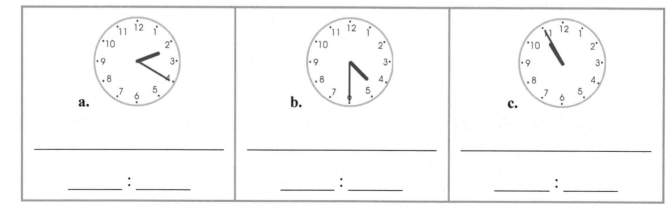

a. _____   _____ : _____

b. _____   _____ : _____

c. _____   _____ : _____

Skills Review 73

1. Divide these shapes.
   Then color.

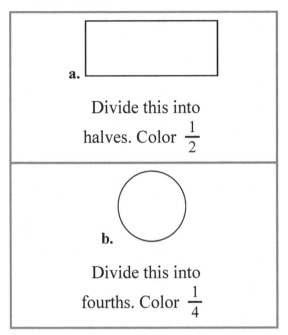

a.

Divide this into

halves. Color $\frac{1}{2}$

b.

Divide this into

fourths. Color $\frac{1}{4}$

2. First, break a ten. Then subtract ones
   and tens separately.

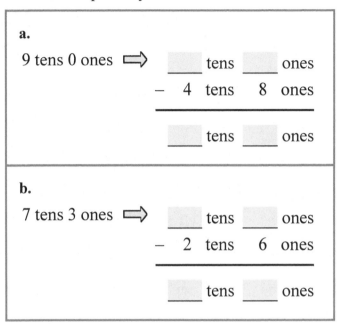

a.

9 tens 0 ones ⟹ ____ tens ____ ones

      –   4   tens   8   ones

       ____ tens ____ ones

b.

7 tens 3 ones ⟹ ____ tens ____ ones

      –   2   tens   6   ones

       ____ tens ____ ones

3. Measure the following things in inches, to the nearest half-inch. Then measure them in
   centimeters, to the nearest whole centimeter. Remember to write "about" if the thing
   is not exactly so many inches or centimeters. Write your results in the table below.

Item	in inches	in centimeters
spoon	in.	cm
shoelace	in.	cm

4. **a.** Eighteen children were playing at the playground.
   Then, twelve more children arrived. How many
   children are at the playground now?

   b. A little later, some of the children had to go home,
   so now there are only twenty-two children at the
   playground. How many children went home?

5. Skip-count.

97, _____, _____, 67, _____, _____, _____, _____, _____

Skills Review 74

1. Add or subtract.

a. 740 + 200 = _____
b. 655 − 300 = _____
c. 483 + 500 = _____

2. Subtract. Check by adding.

a.

$$\begin{array}{r} 5\ 1 \\ -\ 1\ 8 \\ \hline \end{array}$$

Check: + _____

b.

$$\begin{array}{r} 6\ 3 \\ -\ 2\ 9 \\ \hline \end{array}$$

Check: + _____

3. It is 6:30 and Seth just finished planting trees in his orchard. He started planting the trees five hours earlier. At what time did he start planting trees?

4. Write the name of each shape.

a.

_____

b.

_____

c.

_____

d.

_____

e.

_____

f.

_____

5. Which unit would you use to find the following distances: inches (in), feet (ft), or miles (mi)?

Distance	Unit
from Earth to the moon	
the length of a carrot	
the height of a skyscraper	
the distance around a lighthouse	

6. Find one-half of these numbers.

$\frac{1}{2}$ of 14 is _____.
$\frac{1}{2}$ of 22 is _____.
$\frac{1}{2}$ of 50 is _____.
$\frac{1}{2}$ of 48 is _____.

Skills Review 75

1.

May						
Su	Mo	Tu	We	Th	Fr	Sa
1	2	3	4	5	6	7
8	9	10	11	12	13	14
15	16	17	18	19	20	21
22	23	24	25	26	27	28
29	30	31				

Marilyn plays tennis every Wednesday. What dates will she play tennis during the month of May?

May _____   May _____

May _____   May _____

2. Find the total cost.

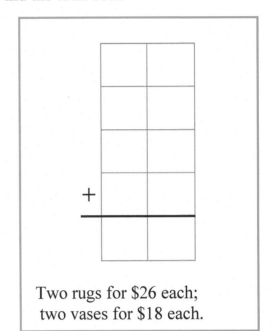

Two rugs for $26 each; two vases for $18 each.

3. Arrange the three numbers in order from the smallest to the largest.

a. 139, 234, 142
b. 851, 784, 890

4. A challenge: figure out the missing numbers! You will need to regroup.

```
  ☐ 0        5 2
- 3 ☐      - ☐ ☐
_____    _____
  5 3        2 7
```

5. Measure the following things using meters and centimeters. First guess how long or tall they are. Then check your guesses by measuring. Let an adult help you.

Item	My guess	How long/tall
broom		
jump rope		
door of your house		

1. Subtract the elevated number in parts. First subtract to the previous whole ten; then the rest.

$$- 7$$
$$/ \quad \backslash$$

a. $41 - \underline{\quad} - \underline{\quad} = \underline{\quad}$

$$- 9$$
$$/ \quad \backslash$$

b. $73 - \underline{\quad} - \underline{\quad} = \underline{\quad}$

2. Fill in the missing numbers.

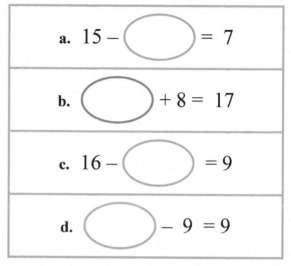

a. $15 - \bigcirc = 7$

b. $\bigcirc + 8 = 17$

c. $16 - \bigcirc = 9$

d. $\bigcirc - 9 = 9$

3. **a.** Weigh yourself with and without a gallon jug of milk or some other liquid.

I weigh _____ lb. I weigh _____ lb with the gallon jug of liquid.

What is the difference? _____ lb.

b. Use the method above with a heavy box. The box weighs _____ lb.

4. Solve.

a. Mrs. Ellis washed 32 towels and hung them on the line to dry. Jimmy's pet goat got loose and pulled 14 of the towels off of the line. How many towels are still hanging on the line?

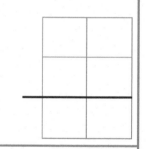

b. Randy's science book has 158 pages, his math book has 160 pages, and his language arts book has 176 pages. How many pages do the three books have in total?

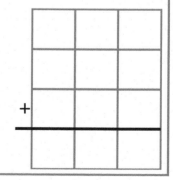

1.

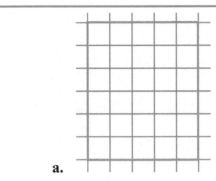

a.
Divide this into thirds. Color $\frac{1}{3}$.

_____ squares in one third

_____ squares in the whole rectangle

b.
Divide this into fourths. Color $\frac{3}{4}$.

_____ squares in three fourths

_____ squares in the whole rectangle

2. **a.** Find out how many kilograms of groceries you can carry in two bags.

I can carry _____ kg of groceries.

  b. Find out how many kilograms of groceries another person can carry and write

the amount here: _____ kg

  c. What is the difference in the weight that you can carry

and the weight that the other person can carry? _____ kg

3. Are these numbers even or odd? Mark an "X". If the number is even, write it as a double of some number.

Number	Even?	Odd?	As a double:
123			
32			
400			
91			

4. Subtract. Regroup if necessary. Find the answers in the line of numbers below.

a.	b.
8 3 − 5 7	6 1 − 3 9
c.	**d.**
3 5 − 1 8	9 8 − 5 7

17 39 26 38 41 18 22

Skills Review 78

1. The bar graph shows how many bottles of juice were sold at a store on a particular day.

   a. How many more bottles of orange juice than pineapple juice did the store sell?

   _____

   b. Make one more question about the bar graph, and solve it. Write it here:

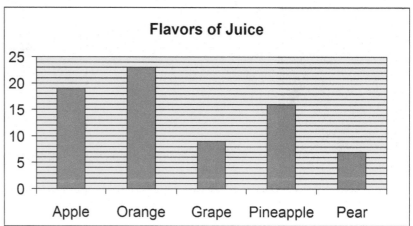

2. To find these differences, think of adding more.

a. 41 − 36 = _____	**b.** 82 − 75 = _____	**c.** 64 − 56 = _____

3. Sharon baked 40 chocolate cookies
   and 24 peanut butter cookies and
   shared them equally with her neighbor.
   How many cookies did each one get?

4. Make these money amounts. Use either real money, or draw. Use at least one quarter.

a. 38¢	**b.** 43¢

Skills Review 79

1. Write how many cents you give, and how many cents is your change.

a.	You give:	Your change:	b.	You give:	Your change:

Price: 55¢ _____ ¢   _____ ¢

Price: 68¢ _____ ¢   _____ ¢

2. Janice borrowed a book from the library
   on Friday and returned it five days later.
   On what day of the week did she return it?

3. Subtract.

a.	b.	c.
5 6 5 − 3 9	7 9 3 − 2 4 7	9 4 1 − 5 2 6

4. Color.

   a. The fifth duck from the left.

   b. The eighth duck from the right.

Puzzle Corner   Figure out the missing numbers for these addition problems.

a.
```
  [ ] 6
+ 1 [ ]
-------
  8 4
```

b.
```
  [ ][ ]
+   8
-------
  6 5
```

c.
```
  4 5
+ [ ][ ]
-------
  9 3
```

d.
```
  3 [ ]
+ [ ] 9
-------
  5 8
```

Skills Review 80

1. The pictograph shows how many pounds of apples different people picked in an orchard.

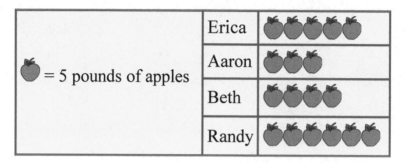

    a. How many fewer pounds of apples did Aaron pick than Randy? _____

    b. How many pounds of apples did Randy, Erica, and Beth pick, in total? _____

2. Draw bills and coins for these amounts.

a. $4.19	**b.** $2.45

3. Draw FOUR dots on the right.
   Connect the dots with straight lines.

   What shape did you draw?

   _____

   It has _____ vertices and _____ sides.

4. Solve.
   Billy and Caleb traveled by car to visit
   their grandma, who lives 513 miles away.
   After traveling 330 miles, they stopped
   at a park. How many more miles did
   they have left to travel?

Skills Review 81

1. Make a line plot for the length of several different small objects, such as a crayon, a toy car, nail clippers, *etc.* Write an "X" mark for each object above the correct number for its length.

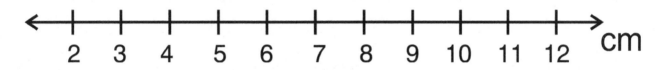

   a. How much shorter is the shortest object than the longest one?

   b. Take four of the objects and put them end-to-end. How long of a line do they make? Add to find out.

   It is _____ cm.   (If you can, measure to check your answer.)

2. Add mentally. Think of the new hundred you get from adding the tens.

   | **a.** $90 + 50 =$ _____ |
   | **b.** $30 + 80 =$ _____ |
   | **c.** $70 + 60 =$ _____ |

3. How many hours is it?

from	3 AM	6 AM	10 AM
to	12 noon	4 PM	2 PM
hours			

4. Find the change. You can draw coins or use real money to help.

a. A key chain: $2.70	**b.** An eraser: $0.47
Customer gives $3.00	Customer gives $1
Change $_____	Change $_____

Skills Review 82

1. Write the time using the expressions "past," "till," or "half past."

 a. 8:55 _____

 b. 1:30 _____

 c. 5:20 _____

2. Add. **a.** $0.37 + $0.89 **b.** $3.76 + $0.09 **c.** $0.58 + $4.19 + $1.83

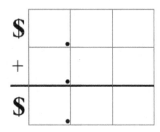 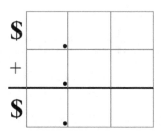 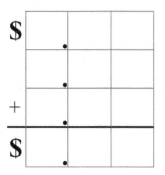

3. Subtract. Check each subtraction by adding.

 a.

 ```
   9 8
 - 2 9          + 2 9
 _____       _____
 ```

 b.

 ```
   7 4
 - 3 8          + 3 8
 _____       _____
 ```

 c.

 ```
   5 5
 - 2 6          + 2 6
 _____       _____
 ```

4. Write the name of the shape. Measure its sides. Find the distance all the way around.

 Side AB _____ inches

 Side BC _____ inches

 Side CD _____ inches

 Side DA _____ inches

 All the way around _____ inches

Skills Review 83

1. Add. Regroup two times if necessary.

a.	b.	c.
6 0 9 + 3 6 1	5 9 8 + 2 4 7	3 3 7 + 3 7 5

2. Write the dollar amount.

a. $_____   b. $_____

3. Circle a suitable weight for each animal.

a.	b.	c.

200 lb 10 lb 900 lb	20 kg 12 kg 2 kg	400 lb 40 lb 4 lb

4. Skip-count backwards.

100, 97, _____, _____, _____, _____, _____, _____, _____

5. Draw the groups. Write the total.

a. 2 × 6 = _____	**b.** 3 × 5 = _____	**c.** 1 × 10 = _____

Skills Review 84

1. Mark went on a trip on March 12th and returned home three weeks later. On what date did Mark return home?

2. Find these differences by adding more.

  a. $43 - 39 = $ _____

  b. $70 - 66 = $ _____

  c. $100 - 93 = $ _____

3. Let an adult help you. Find the distance between two cities, both in miles and in kilometers. Do it for two different locations.

The cities	How many miles	How many km
from to		
from to		

4. Write an addition and a multiplication sentence for each picture.

a.

_____

_____ × _____ = _____

b.

_____

_____ × _____ = _____

5. Draw the coins for the change.

a.  $4.79

Customer gives $5   Change: _____

b.  $1.40

Customer gives $2   Change: _____

Skills Review 85

1. Write the name of the shape. Measure its sides. Find the distance all the way around.

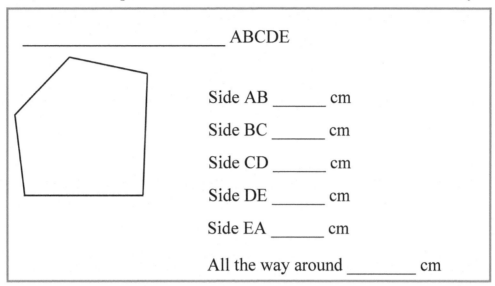

_____ ABCDE

Side AB _____ cm

Side BC _____ cm

Side CD _____ cm

Side DE _____ cm

Side EA _____ cm

All the way around _____ cm

2. Add.

$1.69 + $3.15 + $2.34

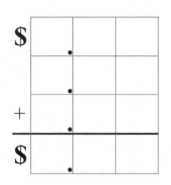

3. Subtract.

a. 7 5 1 − 4 6	**b.** 4 7 0 − 1 3 8
c. 6 8 3 − 2 5 7	**d.** 9 4 2 − 2 1 5

4. Draw jumps to fit the multiplication problem.

```
|--+--+--+--+--+--+--+--+--+--+--+--+--+--+--+--+--+--+--+--+--+--+--+--+--+--+--+--+--+--+--|
0        5         10        15        20        25        30
```

a. $7 \times 2 =$ _____

```
|--+--+--+--+--+--+--+--+--+--+--+--+--+--+--+--+--+--+--+--+--+--+--+--+--+--+--+--+--+--+--|
0        5         10        15        20        25        30
```

b. $4 \times 4 =$ _____

(This page left intentionally blank.)

Printable Shapes

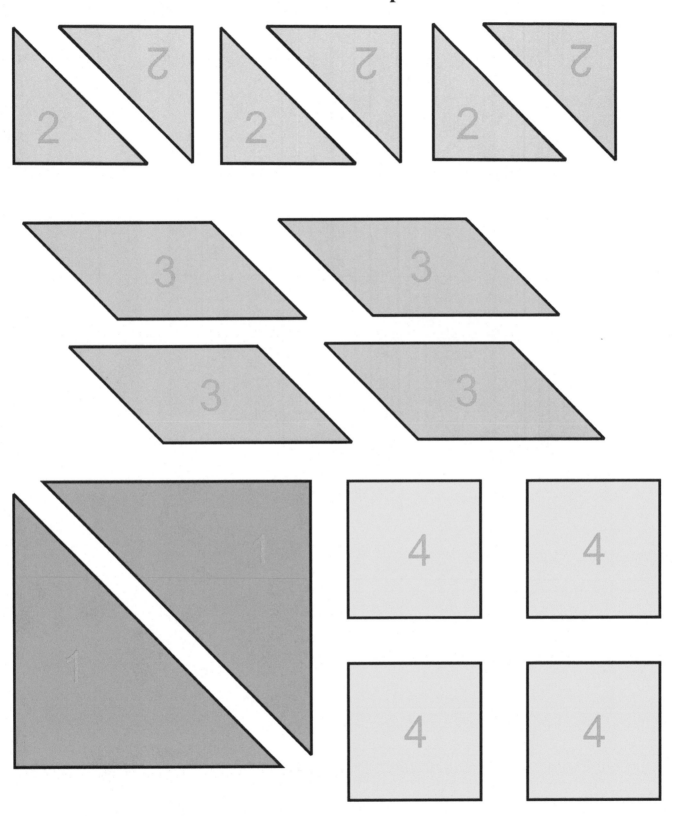

(This page left intentionally blank.)